POCKET
the ∧ decorator

POCKET

the ∧ decorator

By Leslie Banker and Pamela Banker

Illustrations by Kirill Istomin

UNIVERSE

Acknowledgments

Knowledgeable friends, and experts in their respective fields, answered the many questions we had while writing this book. Suzan Cohen of Victor Henschel Floors; architect David McMahon; Alex Carey and Jim Hanley of Taconic Builders; decorative painter Diana Cook Reed; Ramin Hakimi of Ramanan Antique and Decorative Rugs; antique surface restorer Elizabeth Hargraves; Simon Fischer of Versailles Upholstery; John Sullivan of American Silk Mills; and custom lampshade designer Irene Biaggi gave us invaluable information and help.

Our deepest thanks also to Liz Doyle Carey, Lily Malcom, Lela Williams, Lulu Kleinbeck, Helen Marx, Kyra Borré, Robert Mayer, and William Mullins who offered sage advice and support; to Polly Witker for her much needed assistance; to Michelle Coyne, Tracey Holder, Kirill Istomin, Amanda Oakley, and Elisabeth Paton at Pamela Banker Associates for their ongoing help and support; and to The Writers Room for providing a quiet place to work.

A special thank you to our agent Claudia Cross and editor Kathleen Jayes who have been brilliant to work with. Last but not least, much love and many thanks to David Banker for his patience and encouragement.

First published in the United States of America in 2004
by UNIVERSE PUBLISHING
A Division of Rizzoli International Publications, Inc.
300 Park Avenue South
New York, NY 10010
www.rizzoliusa.com

Text © 2003 Leslie Banker and Pamela Banker
Illustrations © Kirill Istomin 2003
Design by Nina Miller Design

2004 2005 2006 2007/ 10 9 8 7 6 5 4 3 2 1

Printed in the United States of America

ISBN: 0-7893-1057-0

Library of Congress Catalog Control Number: 2004104605

contents

Introduction

This book was born of necessity. About five years ago I started working at my mother's interior design firm, Pamela Banker Associates. Although I had a general knowledge of decorating, gained through a lifelong proximity to my mother's work, I was less certain of its specifics. I didn't know the right terms for all the components of interior design, and I also had a lot of questions. How do you know whether to finish a wood floor with wax or with polyurethane? What is the difference between a balloon shade and a Roman shade? When should track lighting be considered? Fortunately, I had a treasure trove of information available in my mother. I began asking questions and keeping a notebook to record what I learned.

The Pocket Decorator is a polished version of that overstuffed notebook. My mother and I worked together, over many cups of tea, to make this a useful resource for any interior design project — from a big house to a small apartment. A lot of design books are big and heavy, not the sort of thing you want to lug around to a meeting with an architect, an upholsterer, or while shopping. We thought this book should be easily tucked into a pocket, a bag, or a briefcase. You'll find vocabulary for specific items as well as practical information, some history, and stylistic ideas. Similar objects are grouped together for easy reference; this is helpful whether you are searching for inspiration or if you only know what something looks like but not what it's called.

For this reason we also wanted the book to be visual, and Kirill Istomin provided beautifully detailed illustrations.

For me, writing this book was a unique opportunity to learn and understand more about what my mother has been doing since before I was even born. We hope that for you this book is an informative guide to creating a house that is as comfortable, practical, and stylish as you want it to be.

Leslie Banker, Spring 2004

Three Guiding Principles of Design

Simplicity, suitability, and proportion are the three guiding principles of interior design. The great twentieth-century decorator Elsie de Wolfe first said this and it still rings true.

SIMPLICITY means less is more. Keep clutter to a minimum. Don't go over the top. A few objects on a tabletop are fine, but too many are distracting.

SUITABILITY means considering how appropriate things are for their use. If you are upholstering a sofa, use a fabric that is strong enough for the job, not a delicate fabric better suited for sheer curtains. Suitability also applies to the stylistic or historic context. It wouldn't be suitable to put a modern chrome and glass coffee table into a Victorian-style living room, for example.

PROPORTION is all about scale. Furniture and objects should be proportional to the room they are in and to each other. You don't want to fill a small room with large armoires and oversized chairs, nor do you want to put a small crown molding into a large room with high ceilings. Save the upholstery fabric with the big, bold print for the big piece of furniture.

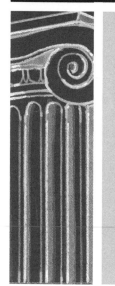

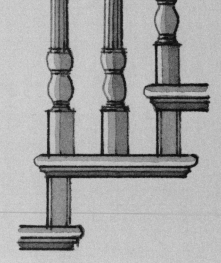

architectural
elements

1

Architectural elements create the character and the look of a house or a room. These elements are the "bones" of a space and include the built-in furniture, doors, moldings, staircases, windows, and overall proportions. In modern architecture of the twentieth century, the elements are spare and pared down without much ornament. In Classical and traditional architecture, the elements are more detailed and elaborate. Many of the architectural elements and the proportions used today are based on Classical architecture.

Basic Architectural Elements

The **CORNICE** is a horizontal projection that provides a transition from the vertical to the horizontal surface where the walls meet the ceiling. A cornice can also be used on the exterior of a building. On the interior a cornice is also called a crown molding and can make a ceiling appear higher.

Cornice is the uppermost section of Classical entablature, which is the area above the columns made up of, from top to bottom, a cornice, a frieze, and an architrave. In Classical architecture the cornice has a series of horizontal sections, and the crown molding is the topmost section of the cornice. Like all moldings, a cornice—or a crown molding—is used to define the space. On an interior wall a cornice can be made from plaster, wood, or, as of recently, a synthetic material.

DADO is the lower third or quarter section of an interior wall that is treated differently from the wall above it. Wood-paneled dadoes, also called wainscot, or tiled dadoes are common. A dado gives a room architectural detail and adds weight and importance. You might use ceramic tiles with a geometric pattern in a dado for a Moorish or Spanish look. A wood-paneled dado has a traditional look. A chair rail, also called a dado cap, is a molding that runs along the top of the dado. A baseboard molding runs along the bottom where the wall meets the floor. It is possible to install just a chair rail and a baseboard and to paint the wall between to simulate the appearance of a traditional dado.

DORMERS are window projections from a pitched roof that have a roof of their own. The roof of a dormer can be gabled, or pitched, at a right angle; it can be curved, which is an eyelid dormer; or it can have a flat slanted roof, called a cat-slide dormer. Inside, dormers add space to a room. They create a nice, cozy nook for a reading chair or a desk. A Roman shade or simple valance with a roller shade underneath are good window treatments for dormers. Also, simple curtains to the windowsill with tie-backs can look very pretty.

ENTABLATURE is the uppermost part of a Classical order of architecture. It is the area above the columns and has three horizontal sections. From top to bottom those sections are: the cornice, the frieze, and the architrave. The cornice is one or a series of horizontal moldings that project from the wall. The frieze is in the middle and can have sculpture in relief, fretwork, be plain, or have a convex curve. The architrave is the molding on the beam that runs over the top of columns to support the entablature. Today full entablature is almost entirely limited to the exterior of buildings. In interiors, you are likely to see only the topmost part of a cornice, which is the crown molding. However, if there are pilasters on the wall, the cornice will be supported by a frieze and an architrave.

FOOTPRINT is the ground area that a building sits on. Footprints are usually mentioned in the context of zoning issues. It might be that the footprint of a new building can only be a certain percentage of the overall size of a lot. Or if you are building an addition, often you can only increase the footprint by a certain percentage.

GABLE is the area beneath a pitched roof that is shaped to the line of the roof. A gable is typically triangular. Buildings, especially in Europe, might have gables with more elaborate shapes or curves. It is common to add a fanlight or a circular window, also called a bull's-eye window, in a gable to add interest to the exterior and bring light to the interior. A gabled roof has two planes pitching downward from a central ridge, thus creating a gable.

ORDERS OF ARCHITECTURE are Classical styles that are differentiated by the design of the columns and entablature and by their proportions. There are five orders of Classical architecture: Composite, Corinthian, Doric, Ionic, and Tuscan. The ancient Egyptians started using stone columns that were carved to resemble tree trunks. The ancient Greeks added fluting to columns and developed the proportions still used widely today. The entablature is the area of the wall above the columns that is divided into three horizontal sections that are from top to bottom: the cornice, the frieze, and the architrave. Columns have, from top to bottom: a capital, a shaft, and a base.

Composite Order is a combination of Corinthian and Ionic Orders and is very elaborate. It is ornate and has the volutes, or spirals, of the Ionic Order and the rows of acanthus leaves of the Corinthian Order. It is a Roman Order of architecture.

Corinthian Order has capitals with two rows of carved acanthus leaves often sprouting four spirals, also called volutes. The Corinthian Order was originally a Greek design but was widely employed later during the Roman Empire. The shaft of the column can be either fluted or not. The Pantheon in Rome has Corinthian capitals.

Doric Order has capitals with a plain curved molding, which is sometimes adorned with a motif. The columns are simple compared to other styles and were used more in ancient Greek architecture than in Roman architecture. The columns are usually fluted though not always. Doric is the oldest of the orders. The Parthenon in Athens has Doric columns.

Ionic Order columns have capitals with two spirals, also called volutes, and shafts that are more slender than Doric columns. The Ionic Order was seen in both Classical Greek and Roman architecture. In Roman architecture the shafts of Ionic Order columns are often plain, with no fluting. In Greek architecture the columns are often fluted. The Temple of Athena Nike in Athens is an example of Ionic architecture.

Tuscan Order is similar to the Doric Order of architecture. The columns are always plain, not fluted, and the proportions are fatter and squatter than in other orders. It was first used by the Etruscans, in the area that is now Tuscany, Italy. It is considered a Roman Order of architecture. It tends to be used on relatively utilitarian buildings.

PEDIMENT is a shaped projection from a wall that is seen over doors or windows. It is a feature of Classical architecture and used often in ancient Greek temples. It can be triangular, curved, or broken, meaning that the topmost section is cut and sometimes is filled with an ornament such as an urn. Pediments are also used in furniture design as a decorative feature on the top of traditional antique forms such as a breakfront, a highboy, or a secretary.

PILASTERS are flat projections from a wall that resemble columns. They are decorative and give interest to an otherwise plain wall. Their proportions are the same as Classical columns. Pilasters are used for punctuation and are seen frequently on either side of a fireplace or a doorway. They are a traditional architectural detail used in more formal settings. They give symmetry to a room; you would not use just one pilaster, but always a pair. Some pilasters extend the full height of a wall, from floor to ceiling, while others just run a portion of the wall. With pilasters, the full Classical entablature is sometimes used, meaning there is an architrave, frieze, and cornice above. Pilasters are often a part of a wood-paneled wall treatment. They can be bought prefabricated from a catalog of wood molding or custom-made.

REVEAL is the cross-section of a wall that is exposed in doorways, windows, or other openings. The deeper a wall, the deeper the reveal will be. Sir John Soane (1753–1837), a brilliant British architect, built bookshelves into the deep reveals of his living room windows at his house in London. This is both practical and adds a great deal of interest to a room. A deep reveal adds dimension and wall surface. If you are building or renovating, try to create deep reveals whenever possible as it adds all sorts of opportunities. Ideally, shutters, blinds, or window shades are installed into the reveal of a window as opposed to on the trim, or surface, of the wall.

SOFFIT is the underside of an architectural element such as an arch, beam, eave, or portico. Kitchen cabinets and lighting fixtures will be installed into a soffit, for example. On the exterior of a house, there is a soffit under the eaves of a roof, which is where the roofline extends beyond the exterior wall of a building.

The **THRESHOLD**, also called the Door Saddle, is the dividing strip of wood or stone in the floor at a doorway. Not every doorway has a threshold as you only need one when the flooring or floor covering changes between rooms. The threshold must be equal in height or slightly higher than the flooring or floor covering. It is often made with beveled edges on one or both sides. If you have wall-to-wall carpeting in one room and a wood floor in the next, you ideally want the threshold to be a half-inch to three-quarters of an inch high on the side with the carpeting and about an eighth of an inch high on the side with the wood floor, which not only looks good but prevents stubbed toes. It is important to make sure new doors clear the threshold.

Built-in Furniture

Built-in furniture has been used in houses for centuries. Early houses had built-in cupboards, niches for displays, and even tables and benches. Other fixtures that can be built-in include window seats, desks, media cabinets, sideboards, chests of drawers, dressing tables, and of course the ubiquitous built-in closet. Built-in furniture adds to the architecture and, since it is generally custom-made to fit into a particular space, will make the most of the room.

BUILT-IN BOOKCASES were seen more frequently starting in the eighteenth century, when houses began to have libraries. Collecting books was a great luxury and built-in bookcases were seen in only the grandest houses. Bookcases were commissioned and designed very elaborately. These days, built-in bookcases are a wonderful addition to a living room, a library, or even a bedroom or hallway. They add to the architecture of a room and can be built to utilize all available space on a wall. Therefore, they can accommodate more books than a separate bookshelf. A cabinet in the lower section, with doors, provides additional storage. This can be a great place to store board games, cards, jigsaw puzzles, and photo albums. A desk can be built into a bookcase, for a home office. Bookcases with open shelves add great warmth and color to a room.

BUILT-IN NICHES are used for displaying collections or decorative objects. They were seen in Classical architecture and have a somewhat formal look. They can be found on both the interior and the exterior of buildings. A niche is often

Some Options for Kitchen Counters

There are many different materials for kitchen counters. Cost, maintenance, appearance, and durability are all considerations. It's important to check with manufacturers about the maintenance and sealing of their materials. The

backsplash, which is the vertical surface behind the countertop, is often finished in the same material as the countertop. Below are a few options:

Glazed Ceramic Tiles are durable and very suitable for a country kitchen.

Solid Synthetics, such as Corian, come in a wide variety of colors and patterns and are highly versatile. They can be used from city to country, informal to formal.

Laminates, such as Formica, are relatively inexpensive and come in many colors and patterns. They are utilitarian, practical, and functional.

Poured Cement countertops have recently become popular. They suit a contemporary look.

Granite, Limestone, and Marble countertops are all very attractive. Granite is the toughest. They are all stylistically versatile.

Stainless Steel requires no sealing, is sleek, contemporary, and utilitarian. It does show finger marks, however.

Wood scratches easily but looks great. The wood should be a hardwood such as maple. It can also be butcher block. Wood countertops work well in a country kitchen. As with all countertops, cutting boards should be used to prevent damage.

fitted with shelves but not always. It is customary to light a niche with display lighting. The interior can be painted the same color as the walls of the room or in a contrasting color. An attractive treatment is to paint the interior a faux stone. In interiors, they are mostly seen in living rooms, dining rooms, hallways, or over a staircase.

Ceilings

A **CATHEDRAL CEILING** follows the roofline and can give a great feeling of open space. The design has been used by architects for centuries and works in the oldest and newest of settings. With a cathedral ceiling you will often see a circular or oval window, also called a bull's-eye window, in the upper portion of the wall. This is a great way to let more light into the room and adds interest to the exterior of the house.

A **TIN CEILING** is made from tiles of tin, which are pressed with patterns. It's a look that was first popular in the U.S. in the late nineteenth and early twentieth century. A tin ceiling is typically seen in loft spaces and bistros, as well as Rocky Mountain saloons. It is best suited to relatively high ceilings. The pressed tin adds texture and has a distinctive historic look. Tin tiles are a good way to cover up a ceiling in disrepair. A note of caution to do-it-yourselfers: tin tiles have sharp edges, and the layout can be difficult to get right. Tin can also be used on walls either just on the lower section or else on the whole wall. Antique tin can be found at salvage shops, and new tin tiles are easily found.

A **TRAY CEILING** is flat at the highest point and angles down to meet the wall. In a renovation, the added height for the ceiling can be carved out of existing attic space. In a room with finished space above, it is impossible to add a tray ceiling. In new construction, a tray ceiling can be an interesting feature to consider, as it adds a feeling of space to a room. The crown molding is applied where the angled sides meet the wall. A hanging light fixture in the center of the ceiling will help the scale of the room. Cove lighting, where light fixtures are installed behind molding at the top of the wall, would also be an option with a tray ceiling.

A **WOOD-BEAMED CEILING** has exposed wooden beams. In the past wood beams were structurally necessary in construction. Today they can be either structural or decorative. They are often seen in the Arts and Crafts style and Mission style of architecture. Wood beams that are rough-sawn or distressed have a more rustic look, whereas more smoothly finished beams look more sophisticated. A farmhouse would typically have a wood-beamed ceiling. The beams can be stained to blend in with the décor or can be painted the same color as the ceiling or the trim. Generally, painting the beams the same color as the ceiling will give the appearance of a higher ceiling.

Doors

Doors are essential for security, privacy, and traffic control. Doors with a flat, or flush, surface are generally seen in modern settings, while paneled doors are more common in traditional interiors.

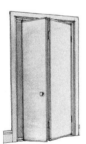

BI-FOLD DOORS are hinged vertically down the middle so they fold in half as they are pulled open. This type of door has a small knob in the center and is mounted on a track attached to the top of the door opening. They can be flush, paneled, or louvered. A bi-fold door is great in a tight space—to conceal a closet or a kitchenette, for instance. The benefit is that when the door is open, it takes up half the space of a standard door. In a small space, another alternative is to hang curtains instead of having a closet door. Lightweight curtains will take up hardly any space when they are open.

A **CONCEALED DOOR**, also called a Blind Door, is finished the same way as the wall. A concealed door is intended to look like a continuation of the wall—as if there is no door at all. The baseboard molding and any other moldings on the wall run across the door. A concealed door is sometimes seen in a wood-paneled room with the paneling continuing across it. Minimal hardware is used. There is no doorknob but an edge pull, which is a flat, slightly curved metal piece affixed to the door inside the seam between the door and wall. The edge pull sticks out just enough to open the door. Pivot hinges or Soss hinges, which are invisible when the door is closed, are used. A concealed door is useful for closet doors in a hallway, or anywhere that a door would detract from the overall design.

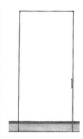

DOUBLE DOORS are two doors hinged on either side of a doorway, opening at the center. French doors are a type of double door. Since a standard single interior door is rarely more than 36 inches wide, double doors are used for wider openings and are often seen between a living room and dining room or on the exterior going out to a deck or terrace. Double doors can be a great way to open up a living space. A pair of narrow double doors at the end of a hallway, for example, can look more symmetrical than a single passage door. In most cases one door is stationary, held by surface bolts on the top and bottom of the door.

DUTCH DOORS are divided horizontally so the lower section can be shut and the upper section left open. The two sections also latch together so the door can open and close as one unit. Generally, Dutch doors are exterior doors. They are versatile as they let in sunlight and air through the upper section, but keep puppies and children contained. A Dutch door works well in a wide variety of situations, but it is closely associated with the country, because barns often have Dutch doors. You could of course put a Dutch door inside a house, in a kitchen or playroom, to keep the wee ones contained and also be able to hear what is going on elsewhere.

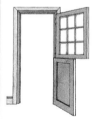

FRENCH DOORS are a hinged pair of double doors with glass panes from top to bottom. First seen in seventeenth-century France, the traditional French door has slender proportions with rather narrow doors. These days, doorways tend to be wider, 5 to 6 feet perhaps, and French doors have expanded proportionally. French doors let in light like a window, and add an elegant touch to a room. You can use them with any style from very sophisticated to traditional. If the ceilings are high enough, a transom, or window (see page 41), over French doors is an excellent way to bring in additional light and open up the wall even more. A cremone bolt is an elegant hardware mount traditionally used on French doors. Surface-mounted bolts, installed at the top and the bottom of the doors, will also do the trick and have a more contemporary look. Curtains can be used with French doors, but must be hung in a way so the doors can be fully operational. A good option is curtains on a pole with rings. Window shades or blinds, if they are required, should be mounted onto the doors.

A **PASSAGE DOOR** is an interior door that is hinged on one side. A traditional passage door is paneled with two, four, six, or more recessed panels, while a more modern door is more likely to be flat, or flush. This basic door comes in a standard height of 6 feet, 8 inches, and the width varies. Passage doors swing in one direction and are thinner and lighter than a typical exterior door. Typically, a passage door opens into the room you are entering; for example, it would open into a bedroom from a hallway and into a bathroom from a bedroom.

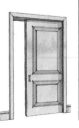

POCKET DOORS are interior sliding doors built into a recess in the wall so when they are open, there is no door visible or taking up space in a room. Pocket doors are absolutely great and suit any style. You can have a single or a double pocket door, and the doors can have traditional details or be flush for a more modern setting. These doors are excellent space savers but require a pocket within the wall. Adding a pocket door is something to consider if you're building or renovating. These doors slide on a track and have a recessed pull instead of a doorknob to open and close the door.

SLIDING DOORS open and close on a track instead of hinging. Common examples are exterior glass sliding doors leading out to a deck or garden, or a pair of solid or louvered sliding closet doors. The chief advantage of sliding doors is that they don't take up floor or wall space when open. Unlike pocket doors, sliding doors will always fill at least half of the doorway. With a sliding door to the exterior you can open it just a crack to let air in and don't have to worry about a door blowing open or slamming shut. In a traditional setting you are more likely to see double or French doors on hinges on the exterior of a house instead of sliding glass doors, which have a more contemporary look.

SWINGING DOORS, or Double-Action Doors, have a special double-action hinge that allows them to swing in two directions. The doors can be any style. Many swinging doors have a small window at eye level, which is useful in a high traffic area. Swinging doors are most often found at the entrance to a kitchen since they can easily be opened when your hands are full. A swinging door is a great convenience, no matter the look of the house. In a more formal dining room, the swinging door leading into the kitchen will often be concealed by a standing screen. These doors don't have knobs but have a push plate set about four feet from the floor to make fingerprints easier to clean. The plate can be metal, glass, or synthetic. A glass or Plexiglas plate is the least obvious.

Fireplaces

Fireplaces are generally the focal point of a room, whether a fire is blazing or not. By about the fourteenth century, in Europe, the fireplace had moved from the center of a great hall over to a wall where a hood channeled smoke out through the wall. Eventually the fireplace was recessed into the wall and vented through a chimney. The mantelpiece became a decorative element.

The **FACING** of a fireplace is a fireproof material—generally stone, brick, metal, or tile—that surrounds the opening on three sides. Facing has to meet building code requirements and varies from about 6 to 12 inches in width depending on the mantel material. The facing should be proportional to the size of the mantelpiece or bolection molding, which is a substantial molding with deep contours that can be used instead of a mantelpiece. You would not want to have a 12-inch-wide facing with a 4-inch-wide mantelpiece or molding. In a country setting, a facing of Mediterranean glazed ceramic tile or brick would be appropriate. Granite with a flamed, or rough, finish has a great rustic look. A more sophisticated look would be marble or limestone, with either a matte or polished finish. In a contemporary setting you might see black stone or metal facing. Delft ceramic tiles, which come from the Netherlands and typically have a white ground with a blue pattern, can make a wonderful facing in either a country or a city setting and have a traditional look. Generally, the facing and the mantelpiece, or molding, don't match. The facing often matches the hearth, although it doesn't have to.

The **HEARTH** is the fireproof area in front of a fireplace that extends into the room. Like the facing, which is the fireproof material around the opening of the fireplace, a hearth is made from stone, brick, metal, or tile. The hearth is generally 12 to 18 inches deep and, like the facing, must meet building code requirements. Generally the hearth and the facing are of the same material, but they don't have to be—it's a matter of choice.

The **MANTELPIECE** frames the facing of a fireplace and is traditionally made from wood or stone and can be highly ornate or very simple. The mantelpiece is often the focal point of a room. It should suit the architecture and the style of the furnishings. The mantelpiece creates a shelf above the fireplace, which is a good place to display objects like an antique clock or a pair of candlesticks. A mirror over a fireplace always looks good. A bolection molding (see page 28) can be used instead of a mantelpiece. This can be less expensive and more flexible as the molding can be cut to any size. Another option is to simply install a shelf, of wood or stone, above the facing. A rough-hewn beam set into the wall above a facing of tiles or brick lends a country look. A polished stone shelf with a facing of stone or metal, on the other hand, looks more modern.

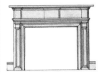

PREFABRICATED FIREPLACES are factory-made and can be installed where there is no existing chimney as they have their own venting system. There are both wood- and gas-burning models. Like all fireplaces, this kind has to meet building code regulations, which vary from location to location. Some buildings have their own restrictions pertaining to prefab fireplaces, so it's best to check. There are different ways a prefab fireplace can vent, through either an exterior wall or a ceiling duct. A fireplace always makes a room feel cozier. If there isn't one in a living room, library, or even a bedroom, it's certainly worth considering putting one in.

WOOD-BURNING STOVES are contained units that are more energy-efficient than an open fireplace. They can be relied on as a heat

source—though it takes work to get a fire going. Wood-burning stoves are made from cast iron; they are functional and not particularly decorative. There are building code specifications for wood-burning stoves that vary from location to location. Some wood-burning stoves have catalytic converters, which boost performance and are therefore more efficient and environmentally friendly.

Wood-burning stoves are definitely rustic looking—perfect in a farmhouse or a country cabin as a supplementary heat source. An interesting alternative to a standard cast iron wood-burning stove is a Swedish ceramic tile stove, which is very pretty and functional. The outside of a Swedish stove is covered in glazed ceramic tiles. The interior has a series of ducts and flues that allow bricks to retain heat from the wood fire below. Swedish stoves are bigger and more difficult to transport than cast-iron stoves.

Heating and Cooling Systems

From an interior design perspective, heating and cooling systems are best when they are not noticeable. It's a good idea to avoid blocking heat and cooling sources. An air conditioner or a heater will be less effective if a sofa is placed right in front of it, and carpeting should be cut around air vents in the floor.

BASEBOARD HEATING runs along the bottom of the wall. It can be hooked into either a central hot water heating system or a local electric heater. It's not a good idea to have curtains fall over a baseboard heater. Curtains to the windowsill, window shades, or blinds are a better option. The curtains will trap heat and can be discolored over time— it can also be a fire hazard. Likewise, baseboard heating will affect your furniture layout as you don't want to put sofas and upholstered chairs directly up against it.

CEILING FANS require a relatively high ceiling. In hot climates, a ceiling fan generates a constant breeze. In cooler climates, it is used to push warm air down to the floor level. The power source is an electrical box in the ceiling. If there is an existing electrical box, there is often a visible cap. Otherwise, an electrician will have to cut a hole in the ceiling to find an electrical line. A brace to support the weight of the fan will also have to be installed—in most situations. Ideally, the fan is operated with a wall switch, which the electrical box in the ceiling is connected to. It is also possible to run a wire on the wall and ceiling, but it looks best if it's wired directly into the ceiling, and therefore unseen. A ceiling fan can be annoying if it's over a place where you do paperwork.

CENTRAL SYSTEMS have either heating or cooling capabilities or both. They can heat and cool the house as a whole or by zones. There are a number of types of systems. Heating and cooling can be delivered through air vents, or heat can be delivered through hot water or steam systems. It's a good idea to have an annual service contract for your central heating or cooling systems. Systems with air ducts will have filters that should be cleaned regularly to keep dust and dirt from being recirculated though the house.

RADIANT HEATING SYSTEMS have tubing filled with hot water embedded in the walls, ceilings, or floors either throughout the house or just in specific rooms. Electrical heating components, instead of tubing filled with hot water, can also be used in a radiant heating system. With radiant heat the air in a room is not warmed up so much as the objects—including people and furniture. Radiant heating systems deliver heat evenly through a room. Also, they do not affect your furniture layout and aren't visible.

Radiant heating systems are known to be fuel-efficient, though the installation can be expensive.

In new construction or a renovation, radiant heat should be considered. Some radiant systems can also be used for cooling, but are generally separate from the heating system. Basically any floor covering can be used with radiant heat, as the floor does not get very hot. It's a good idea to double check though. A cast iron radiator is a form of radiant heat, but it operates at much higher temperatures than systems set into the floors, walls, or ceilings.

RADIATORS can be heated with either steam or hot water. They are typically made of cast iron and get very hot to the touch. Ideally, radiators are concealed as they are not very attractive. Radiator covers with grilles for the heat to escape through can be built or bought pre-made. These covers can also double as a window seat or an extension of the windowsill. A radiator cover should be painted the same color as the wall or as the trim. You can also use lattice set in a frame for a radiator cover. The covers must be movable for maintenance. There are new designs for radiators that are more attractive than the old standard.

THROUGH-WALL UNITS, as the name implies, go through the wall, often below a window. These units can be combination heating and cooling or cooling only. They can be electric or be hooked into a steam system. The unit fits into a sleeve, which then fits into a hole in the wall. The advantage of a through-wall air conditioner is that it will not take up valuable window space and is less ugly than a window air conditioner. Installation will require opening the wall to insert a sleeve to hold the unit.

A **WINDOW AIR-CONDITIONING UNIT** is the most versatile as it fits into a window and can be removed when it's no longer needed. The downside is that it obscures a view out the window and is not beautiful to look at from the outside.

However, it requires no construction and in many situations is the only solution. Since a window unit does block the view, think about storing it in the winter if it's not needed. Window air-conditioning units are far better suited to double-hung windows than casement windows.

Moldings

Moldings are a detail of great importance, especially in Classical architecture and period styles. The basic purpose of moldings is to create shadow and definition on a surface, to highlight or separate elements, to cover seams, and to provide decorative detail. Moldings are made of wood, plaster, or, as of recently, a synthetic material. Some moldings have a contoured profile while others have a flush, or flat, profile. When choosing moldings, pick ones that are in keeping with the architecture and style of the room. Also, the size of the moldings should be proportional to the room — a wide molding for a larger space and a narrow molding in a smaller space. Moldings can be found in millwork catalogs and home furnishing outlets or can be custom-milled by a cabinetmaker. Moldings are traditionally used in the following ways, but they can be applied successfully to other areas as well.

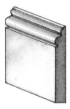

ASTRAGAL is a symmetrical molding that is frequently applied to the edge of a door to keep out light and drafts. On a pair of double doors, the astragal would be applied to the vertical edge of one door to cover the gap or space where the two doors meet. The word astragal is derived from the Greek *astragalos*, meaning a molding. A small astragal molding could also be used as muntin bars, which separate the panes in a window. In Classical architecture an astragal is also a band of molding used around the top of a column.

BASEBOARD is the molding that runs along the wall at floor level defining the bottom of the wall. The size of the baseboard should be proportional to the height of the ceiling and to other moldings in the room. Generally speaking, in a traditional setting with an average ceiling height, the baseboard molding is about 6 inches high — a 4-inch square with a 2-inch cap. In a more modern setting you would use a 2- to 4-inch-high square baseboard and leave off the 2-inch cap. When the floor is uneven, there might be a gap between the bottom of the baseboard and the floor along some parts of the wall, in which case a quarter round shoe molding should be used. Changing a typical small baseboard to a more significant baseboard can make a big aesthetic difference.

BOLECTION MOLDING, also called Mantel Molding, is often used instead of a mantelpiece to frame the facing around a fireplace. It is also used in wood paneling to cover a joint between uneven surfaces. It is a substantial molding with deep contours and profile. When used instead of a mantelpiece, bolection molding is suitable in either a traditional or a contemporary setting and is less ornate and typically less expensive. It can be painted or stained with the wall or else picked out in a contrasting color to the wall along with the other moldings in the room. Also, it can be painted with a decorative finish such as faux wood or stone. When you use bolection molding instead of a mantelpiece, there will be no shelf created above the fireplace. It is possible to affix the bolection molding onto a board to create a narrow shelf above the fireplace as a place to display decorative objects.

A **CHAIR RAIL**—also called a Dado Cap or a Dado Rail—is installed horizontally around a room approximately 32 inches from the floor. In Europe in the seventeenth and eighteenth centuries, chairs in a formal room were often placed against the walls instead of scattered throughout the room. Originally, chair rails protected the walls from being damaged by the backs of chairs. It is generally 2 to 3 inches wide with a contoured profile. Like other moldings, it adds an architectural detail to a room. It has a particularly traditional look and defines the space above and below it. If the wall below the chair rail is treated differently from the wall above, then the lower section is called the dado. If there is wallpaper or a mural only on the upper section of a wall, then you'll need a chair rail to separate it from the wall below. A wallpaper or stenciled border design can be used instead of a chair rail for the same purpose.

CORNER BLOCKS, or Rosettes, are installed at the corners of window and door casing. With corner blocks, the window and door casing is often fluted. The combination of the fluted casing and corner blocks provides a good finished frame

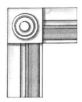

that can eliminate the need for curtains. A motif is almost always carved into them—a bull's eye or simple flower is typical. Corner blocks can be successful in a variety of traditional situations. They were seen in eighteenth- and nineteenth-century England and America in the Georgian and Federal styles. When corner blocks are used with door casing, it is almost always in conjunction with a plinth block, which is a molding at baseboard level that acts as a visual support for the door casing.

COVE MOLDING, also called Cavetto, is a Classical concave molding with simple lines that is a type of crown molding used at the juncture of the wall and the ceiling. Like other types of crown molding, cove molding can create the appearance of a higher ceiling. A 3- to 6-inch cove molding is generally used. The size should be proportional to the size of the room. The shape of the cove molding is so simple that it works very well with a wide variety of looks and is a good option when mixing styles.

CROWN MOLDING is installed at the junction of the wall and the ceiling. In Classical architecture a crown molding is the uppermost part of the cornice. A 3- to 6-inch crown molding is generally used and, as with all moldings, the size should be proportional to the size of the room. There are many different profiles to choose from, some more elaborate than others. Crown molding can be a relatively inexpensive facelift for a room, providing an architectural touch to an otherwise plain room. It appears to increase the height of a ceiling. In a more streamlined setting, you might use a cove molding or do without crown molding.

DENTIL MOLDING is a horizontal series of square blocks that go under the cornice, or crown molding, to add detail and break up the shadow thrown by the molding above. The name dentil is thought to come from the French word *dent*, meaning tooth. A row of dentil molding indeed does resemble a row of wide-spaced teeth. It is an element of Classical architecture seen throughout the ages on the interior and exterior of buildings as well as on furniture. Dentil molding comes in a wide variety of scales, and the size of the molding should be relative to its surroundings. It is an interesting addition and is generally used in more formal settings.

DOOR AND WINDOW CASING—also known as the Architrave—frames windows and doors or any opening in a wall. In much twentieth-century construction, window and door casings are metal instead of the more traditional wood frames. Adding a wood casing over a metal casing can give an architectural significance to a space. Door and window casing might also be used to frame a pass-through between a kitchen and a dining room, for example, or on built-in cabinet-work. It is sometimes used with corner blocks at the corners and plinth blocks at the baseboard.

PICTURE MOLDING is a narrow molding installed at the ceiling line or on the wall about 2 to 3 feet below the ceiling and used to hang pictures. Museums, galleries, and private collections use it for added flexibility as it means that nails do not have to be hammered into the walls. The pictures hang from a rod or a wire that hooks around the picture molding. When you use picture molding for hanging pictures, you will see the rod that the picture is hanging on.

PLINTH BLOCK is used at baseboard level below door casing, and sometimes window casing. The plinth block acts as a visual support for the casing. In Classical architecture the plinth is the slab beneath the base of a column or a pedestal. Plinth blocks are often used in a traditional setting, and they are sometimes carved with a simple motif. They add architectural detail to a room—no matter the setting. Plinth blocks protect the door and window casing from being damaged by, for example, vacuum cleaners. It's easier to repaint a plinth block than to have to repaint a whole door casing. Plinth blocks are finished with the baseboard.

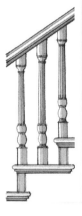

SHOE MOLD is a quarter round molding that hides the gap between the baseboard and the floor if the floor is uneven. The top edge of a baseboard must be level on the wall, so if the floor slants, a gap will be created. Shoe molding fills that gap. It should not be used where carpeting is being installed wall to wall. It is a much neater installation for carpet to go right to the baseboard and not to a shoe mold.

Staircases

The staircase has always been a very important architectural statement. The design and shape of the staircase is limited by the height of the ceilings and the available space.

BALUSTERS are the vertical supports for a handrail. A row of balusters is called the balustrade. Early balusters were often made from turned wood. By the late eighteenth century, iron balusters were frequently used. Beautiful ironwork balustrades are seen in Spanish styles. In Modern architecture in the twentieth century, the balustrade often had horizontal elements running parallel to the handrail. Today there is a wide array of choice from turned wood to metal cable. Balusters can either be set directly onto the tread, the horizontal part of the step, which is called open string (illustrated here), or they can be set onto a diagonal brace, which is called closed string. Balusters are also seen on balconies and incorporated into furniture design.

The **HANDRAIL** on a stair is supported by the balustrade and is 32 to 36 inches high and made of wood, metal, or occasionally, in a formal setting, of stone. A handrail can also be made from a sturdy rope, velvet-covered or not, supported by brackets on a wall. In a cottage by the sea it could be quite charming to have a real hemp rope attached to the wall as a handrail. More ornate handrails might end in a spiral around the newel post, while less elaborate handrails are simply functional. No matter what the handrail looks like, it always serves a function, which is to help keep people from falling down the stairs.

NEWEL POSTS are the vertical supports for the handrail at the top and the bottom of a staircase or at a point where the stairs change direction. They are structurally necessary to support the handrail. For centuries newel posts have been elaborately designed. They do not have to be elaborate, though—a simple post also does the

Recycled and Salvaged Materials

The perfect material or fixture is not always brand new. If you are fixing up an older house, or trying to create the appearance of age in a newer house, it's worth looking into salvaged or recycled materials. In some situations you may want to use salvaged wood floorboards or barn siding to panel a room. A vintage clawfoot bathtub could be just perfect in an older house.

Architectural salvage shops also sell old hardware, lighting, and plumbing fixtures. You might find that authentic Art Nouveau light fixture you've been looking for or terra-cotta floor tiles from a villa in Italy. Doors, hinges, doorknobs, iron gates, windows, and fire screens are some other things you might find. It's important to carefully inspect the condition of salvaged items before buying them. Salvaged goods are not necessarily less expensive than new items; in fact, they can be more expensive as they have the cachet of age.

trick. Traditionally, a newel post is topped off with a finial, which is an ornamental knob used at the top of a pole or post. Newel posts through the centuries have been a particularly important architectural detail. Even relatively modest houses had elaborately carved newel posts.

Windows

AWNING WINDOWS are horizontal rectangles hinged along the top so they open up and out. They were first seen in the early twentieth century and usually have just one pane of glass. It's possible to stack awning windows on top of each other or to install a series of them side by side. Placed high on a wall they bring light and ventilation into a room while maintaining privacy. Awning windows open and close using a crank at windowsill level. When installing the windows high on a wall, consider whether you will be able to reach the crank. Awning windows often require no window treatment or else something simple such as a basic shade.

BAY WINDOWS project from the face of a building and are built at ground level with a roof above. They generally have three flat sides. Architects today use them quite frequently as they are suitable for almost any type of building, from traditional to contemporary. Bay windows add square footage and light to a room. The additional space is great for a built-in window seat or a seating area with a table and chairs; and the windows themselves can be double-hung, casement, or picture windows. Window shades, rather than curtains, are more functional in a bay window. You can hang stationary curtain panels on the face of the wall with a curtain pole running across the top of the opening. It is more difficult to hang curtains inside the angled bay. A bay window supported on brackets, generally seen on the second floor, or higher, is called an oriel window.

BOW WINDOWS are projections from the face of a building that are similar to bay windows except that bow windows are curved and bay windows have flat planes. Like a bay window, a bow window adds space and light to a room and is conducive to a window seat or a dining table. They are a little more elegant—and more expensive—than bay windows. Curtains can be hung from one curved track in a bow window. Alternatively you can hang stationary curtain panels on the face of the wall with a curtain pole running across the top of the opening. Because of the curve, window shades are difficult in a bow window.

CASEMENT WINDOWS are hinged on the side of the window frame and swing either out or in to open. The first windows to open and close were casements. They are typical of the Tudor style from the sixteenth and seventeenth centuries, with small panes of leaded glass set on the diagonal. Today casement windows can have one pane of glass or multiple panes. They are opened using a crank at windowsill level. They are great in tall narrow spaces and work well with both modern and traditional styles. They are very versatile. If the windows open into the room, then your choice of window treatments will be limited. There are more window treatment choices with windows that open out. Double-hung windows are a bit more versatile than casements as they can open wide or just a crack from either the top or the bottom. Over a kitchen sink, however, it is easier to crank open a window than to lean over and raise it. Window air-conditioning units are a problem with casement windows.

CIRCULAR WINDOWS and **OVAL WINDOWS** are also called Bull's-Eye Windows. They can be fixed, meaning they don't open, or operable. Circular and oval windows are typical of Baroque architecture. These windows have also been used with many other styles—from

American Colonial architecture to Modern architecture of the twentieth century. Some circular windows have one pane of glass while others are more stylized with many panes. Traditionally they had many panes of glass with decorative muntin, or glazing, bars separating the panes. Architecturally, circular windows add interest to the exterior of a building, and are often used for that purpose. You'll find them centered over a front door or in a gable, the shaped area below a roofline. These windows are great for bringing light into a room and breaking up a wall that is unusually high, such as below a cathedral ceiling. There is rarely a need for a window treatment on a circular, or oval, window.

CLERESTORY WINDOWS are windows installed either high on a wall near the ceiling or else in a section of wall that extends above the surrounding roof. Clerestory refers to the placement of the window and not the style, though clerestory windows are often fixed, meaning they don't open. The word clerestory comes from Middle English meaning "clear story" and this use of windows can be seen often in very old churches but also in recent architecture. The twentieth-century American architect Frank Lloyd Wright, for example, used clerestory windows, sometimes in stained glass. The effect is much like a skylight. If you are building a house or renovating, adding clerestory windows can be a great idea, especially for rooms that will be used during the daytime. They do require a high ceiling, though. Since the purpose of clerestory windows is to let in light and because they are up high on a wall, no window treatment is necessary.

DOUBLE-HUNG WINDOWS have two sashes that slide up and down vertically. The first windows with two sashes were developed in Europe in the late seventeenth century and were widely used in both Europe and America by the early to mid-eighteenth century. The first double-hung windows had multiple panes of glass in each sash. As it became possible to make larger pieces of glass, windows were made with fewer panes. Modern windows often have just one large pane in each sash.

When you hear a window described as "four over four," it means there are four panes of glass in each sash. Historic houses that have been preserved in their original form often have "twelve over twelve" windows, sometimes with the original leaded glass—which adds interesting irregularities in tint and texture. On some windows made today, the muntin bars, which divide the panes of glass, don't serve a function but just snap on to simulate a more traditional look. Newly manufactured double-hung windows can be tilted open inward for easy cleaning. This is convenient, especially for windows on the second floor or higher. Compared to casement windows, which open like a door, double-hung are more versatile. They can be opened from the bottom or the top, either a little bit or a lot. Any type of window treatment works with double-hung windows. They can easily hold an air conditioner.

FANLIGHTS have a curved shape, like a fan, and are generally fixed, meaning they don't open. Historically, fanlights had intricately designed muntin bars, also called glazing bars, which hold the panes of glass in place. They are seen above doors, on their own, and frequently in a gable. They are a type of transom—a window above a door—and their purpose is similar to a circular or oval window in that they are often used to create detail on the exterior of a building. Today fanlights are available in standard sizes, or can be custom-made. Also, old fanlights can be found at antique or salvage shops and can sometimes be installed as working windows or just hung indoors on a wall as an ornamental piece. This can be very pretty.

GLAZING is the glass used in windows and doors. Glass has been made for thousands of years, but the process of making flat, clear panes suitable for windows took a long time to develop. Prior to glass panes, there were just holes in the walls that were covered by shutters. Glass panes were initially small and opaque. They were made by spinning a tube of glass which was then cut open and laid flat. Over time glass production techniques improved, and the panes increased in size, culminating in the picture windows of the nineteenth and twentieth centuries. In 1834 an Englishman named Robert Lucas Chance made panes of glass that were larger and clearer than they had been before. He supplied the glass for the Crystal Palace at the Great Exhibition of 1851 in London, which drew huge crowds and was an early example of a prefabricated building. The Crystal Palace was made primarily of glass.

It used to be that windows had just one layer of glass per pane, which is called single glazing. Now windows have a double layer of glass, called double glazing, which creates an insulating air pocket. The names and technologies vary from company to company, but some insulated windows have a coating on the glass to increase their effectiveness. Using storm windows in the winter is a simple form of double glazing; although the air pocket is not sealed, it offers some insulation. For areas prone to hurricanes and harsh storms, there are windows made with impact-resistant glass. Some types of glazing offer ultraviolet light protection. Building codes often require that glazing be insulated.

MULLION is the vertical post that divides a window or an opening. If you have two or more casement windows together in an opening, there will be a mullion between them. Mullions are made from stone, wood, or metal.

MUNTIN BARS, also called Glazing Bars, are what hold the panes of glass into a window sash. Originally it wasn't possible to make very large panes of glass. Centuries ago, windows had many small panes of glass and therefore more muntin bars. As technology progressed it became fashionable to have larger panes of glass and fewer and thinner muntin bars. By the early nineteenth century, relatively large panes of glass were available. Muntin bars can be quite decorative. In a fanlight, which is a semicircular stationary window, the muntin bars and panes of glass can be made in beautifully shaped designs. Today windows are often made with just one pane of glass and have snap-on muntin bars to make them appear more traditional. In a more contemporary setting, windows would have no muntin bars.

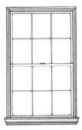

PALLADIAN WINDOWS have a central arched window with a tall narrow window on either side. Also called Venetian windows, they provide a focal point in a room and on the exterior of a building. They are named after the Italian architect Andrea Palladio (1508–1580), whose work is the basis of the Palladian style of architecture. Palladio based his style on Classical architecture, and some well-known examples of his work, such as the Villa Capra in Italy, are still standing today. Palladio's work has been very influential over the centuries. Palladian windows were often used in seventeenth- and eighteenth-century English architecture, in American Colonial architecture, and they are widely seen today. They have a grand look. The size of the window needs to be scaled to the size of the room. A window treatment is not always necessary on a Palladian window.

PICTURE WINDOWS are single panes of stationary glass that can be quite large. They offer a big view and give lots of light—the important thing is to love the view. A large picture window helps to bring the exterior in. The window treatment could be a Roman shade, a wood or metal blind, or a simple pair of curtains. In some cases the best solution is to have no window treatment. A picture window can be flanked by smaller windows that are operable. Birds sometimes fly into picture windows. You can deter them by moving bird feeders away from the window, especially during migration seasons.

SIDELIGHTS are fixed panels installed on either side of an exterior door. They have been used for centuries and can be any style. They have either one single pane or multiple panes of glass, and can stop at the windowsill level or extend the full height of the door. Sidelights have the effect of making an entryway grander and bringing more light into an entry hall. Many exterior doors can be bought with sidelights in a complementary style. Sidelights also mean you can see outside without opening the door.

A **SKYLIGHT** is basically a window installed into a roof. There are a wide variety of options when choosing a skylight. It can be stationary or operable. Some models open and close the skylight with a remote control, and some are outfitted with rain sensors so they close on their own at the first drop. Use skylights in situations where there is no room on a wall for a window or else in an interior room such as a bathroom or a hallway. In a room with windows, a skylight offers even more natural light. There are window shades made for skylights that will help to keep direct sunlight out. Installing a skylight is not terribly complicated, and it can make a big difference in a small, dark room. One thing to note is that light coming through a skylight is not as easily controlled as with a window.

STAINED GLASS has pigments baked or fused into the glass that give it color. Cathedrals in Europe dating at least back to the twelfth century have exquisite stained-glass windows. Chartres Cathedral in France has beautiful early stained-glass windows. Stained glass also has had a long presence in secular life. During the early nineteenth century, it was fashionable to have stained-glass strips incorporated into clear glass windows. The twentieth-century architect Frank Lloyd Wright often used stained glass, and the Tiffany Studios in New York made beautiful windows. Besides windows, Tiffany Studios also made lighting fixtures using stained glass.

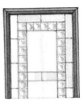

TILT AND TURN WINDOWS open two ways: on a vertical pivot, like an inward swinging door, or on a horizontal pivot, tilting in about 6 inches from the top. They have one single pane of glass and a handle on the side that regulates which way the window opens. Tilt and turn windows are most often seen in apartment buildings. When they are tilted open, air comes in through the top and sides. When they are swung open like a door for cleaning, it hinges so both sides of the window can be easily reached. These windows are a challenge for window treatment. The best solution is either shades attached directly to the window or curtains on a pole.

A **TRANSOM** is a window above a door that can be either stationary, movable, or have louvers. A fanlight is a type of transom. Transoms were used before air conditioning so you could close a door to a room but still have air circulation. They let in additional light, give height to a window or door, and open up a wall. In a room with high ceilings, adding a transom can be an excellent idea. Transoms work very well over French doors. A transom, by definition, is also a horizontal bar across the top or middle of a window—the architectural opposite of a mullion (see page 38).

fabrics

2

When choosing a fabric for decorating purposes, one of the first things to consider is its suitability. Is it sheer enough to be a sheer curtain? Will it hang and drape well for curtains? Is it sturdy enough for upholstery? Will it wash well enough to be a slipcover? Will it show dirt if it's on a sofa that is used every day?

Fabric Types

BATIKS are made using a wax-resistant dye technique that originated in Java. To make batik, fabric is painted or stamped with melted wax. The fabric is immersed in a dye bath and the waxed areas resist the dye. The wax is removed using heat, typically from an iron. Batiks have a very Eastern, casual look that goes well with bamboo and rattan furniture. The colors are usually strong and deep, primary or earthy, and can evoke the feeling of a bungalow in Bali. Batiks are traditionally thinner fabrics, such as cotton or silk, that are great for throw pillows, bedspreads, or unlined curtains blowing in the breeze. These fabrics are not generally strong enough for upholstery. The batik effect is also replicated by machine; this can be done on heavier fabrics suitable for upholstery.

BROCADE has a raised pattern, often floral, woven into the background fabric, typically silk. Early brocades were made in China. Persia, now Iran, has a long history of making beautiful silk brocades, often with gold and silver threads. Brocade was particularly popular in sixteenth- and seventeenth-century Europe in the grandest of situations—in palaces and royal courts. Brocade was originally hand-embroidered, but is now almost always machine-made using a jacquard loom attachment, which gives it the look of hand embroidery. It is very elegant, special, and a rather fancy fabric. You might find brocade on curtains, valances, table skirts, a fancy bed canopy, or on a fine French chair. It is not suitable for constant wear and tear.

BURLAP is a coarse, loosely woven fabric usually made from jute or hemp. It is very basic; the stuff sacks are made of. It is used in the construction of upholstery to cover the springs of a piece of furniture. Burlap can add great texture when it is applied to a surface—stretched over a simple wood table, for example—and painted. Burlap is also printed or painted to be a primary fabric. It has a rustic look.

CALICO is a plain-woven cotton fabric often printed with a small-scale floral design. The word comes from Calicut, a city in southwestern India from where calico was originally exported. Calico has a simple charm suitable for a country house. You could use calico on a bedspread, an upholstered headboard, or a bedskirt. It can also be used for curtains—windowsill-length calico curtains could go in a country kitchen, bedroom, or bathroom.

CHENILLE is an elegant and stylish woven fabric made from silk, cotton, rayon, or wool yarn that has protruding pile on all sides. Chenille is one of the best upholstery fabrics as it feels good and is durable. The word *chenille* is French for "caterpillar," which is an apt description of the yarn. It is an all-around great fabric that goes with a wide variety of looks and can be dressed up or dressed down. Banquettes, chairs, and sofas can all be upholstered in chenille.

CHINTZ is a cotton fabric that originated in India in the 1600s. The name is derived from the Hindi word *chint*, meaning "spotted." Originally used in eighteenth-century English and European houses, it also found great favor in the U.S. In the 1980s there was a chintz craze—it was being used everywhere, from beds to sofas to lampshades, and all at once. These days, it is still widely used, but with greater moderation. The fabric often has a printed floral design but can also be a solid color. It is almost always glazed, which protects it from dirt and gives it a shine. For pattern and color, in a room with a classic look, there is nothing prettier than a printed chintz. It can be used for almost anything: curtains, upholstered furniture, pillows, bedspreads, and bedskirts. Solid chintz is often used as a line of color to trim lampshades, bedskirts, tablecloths, and curtains. Chintz can be used for upholstered walls or paperbacked and hung as wall covering. The fabric can be either hand-blocked or machine printed; hand-blocked is more expensive. Chintz will eventually lose its glaze from wear and cleaning, but nothing is nicer than an old faded chintz. Vintage chintz can be bought through antique textile dealers.

CORDUROY is a heavy fabric with vertical ribs of cut pile. It is commonly used for clothing but is also a great upholstery fabric. The ribs add an interesting design element and texture, and the fabric is soft and durable. The ribs can vary in width from very narrow to quite wide. You might use corduroy with wide ribs on a sofa in a traditional library. Corduroy can also be used successfully in a contemporary setting.

CREWELWORK refers to cotton or linen fabric embroidered with wool, typically in floral patterns. The word comes from the late Middle English word *crule*, meaning "yarn." Its origins are English dating to approximately the early seventeenth century. The embroidered design does not cover the entire fabric, so the cotton or linen background will show through. Crewelwork can be used for upholstery, curtains, or as a bedspread. Since the embroidery work generally creates a large-scale pattern, you would not want to obscure the pattern with tufting or channeling in upholstery. You might also consider using crewelwork on a throw pillow or as a wall hanging. It is still handmade today, and if you are interested in doing crafts at home, there are kits for making crewelwork. Also, there are some beautiful antique pieces of crewelwork.

DAMASK is a woven fabric with a pattern that is generally matte against a shiny background. It is created using a jacquard loom attachment. The pattern and the background are often the same color, but have different weaves. The name comes from the city of Damascus, Syria, where the fabric was first made. It is traditionally made from silk, but is now found in cotton, linen, rayon, or a combination of fibers. It is elegant, formal, and classic. Damask works well for lined curtains and for upholstery. As with brocade, you use damask in a formal room that does not get a lot of wear and tear.

GINGHAM is a lightweight cotton with a pattern woven into the fabric. It is the classic red or blue-checked tablecloth fabric but is also found in stripes and plaid. It has an informal country look and can be used for kitchen curtains and, of course, for tablecloths. Loose seat cushions on a wooden chair can be made from gingham. It also works for upholstery, a headboard, or throw pillows.

HAND-BLOCK PRINTS are made with the centuries-old technique of printing fabric with wooden blocks. Each color in the design requires a separate woodblock. The vertical repeat can be any size on a hand-block print, unlike fabrics printed by machine. Hand-blocking is very time consuming; therefore, fabric made this way is generally more expensive than prints produced by machine. Printing by hand shows imperfections and inconsistencies that add to the unique quality of each piece of cloth. The tone and depth of the dye will vary depending on how hard the printer presses down, and there will always be

Cuttings For Approval and Repeats

Cuttings for approval

When ordering fabric, be sure you get a cutting of the current stock. The color of a fabric can vary quite significantly from dye lot to dye lot.

Repeats

In a patterned fabric, wall covering, or carpeting there is a repeat. This means that at regular intervals (every 5 inches or 30 inches, for example), the pattern is repeated. With a larger repeat you will need to order extra yardage.

This is because when upholstering you want the pattern to be centered on all the cushions even though there will be some waste, which can sometimes be used on borders. When hanging wallpaper, the pattern must fall at the same point on every wall. With a larger repeat, some paper will be wasted to make this happen.

slight variations as the design is repeated along the length of the fabric. If budget allows, these fabrics are works of art.

HORSEHAIR CLOTH is a strong fabric that is woven with horsehair filler and a cotton or linen warp. In French it is called *le crin,* which means "horsehair." Crinoline used for women's petticoats in the nineteenth century was originally made with horsehair, and horsehair is still used today as padding for clothing as well as in upholstery. Horsehair cloth for decorating is either a solid color, striped, or patterned with a small motif. Horsehair cloth is very chic, stylish, and durable. It comes in a narrow width so multiple seams are often required when using it for upholstery. Unlike chenille, it is not soft and cozy but rather stiff and formal. Upholstered on a bench or the seat of a chair it looks great — you might cover the seat of a settee with horsehair. You would not use it for curtains or anywhere fabric needs to drape well.

LACE is an ornamental openwork fabric made originally from threads that are looped, knotted, and twisted by hand using tools such as needles, bobbins, and bones. Starting in the late eighteenth century to early nineteenth century lace also was made by machine. Belgium and Italy are both known for their early contributions to the history of lace starting in about the fifteenth century. Lace was originally made as a trimming for clothing and later for decorative items such as curtains and tablecloths. Early lace was made from linen, then cotton was used, and now it is made with both natural and synthetic fibers. It can be incredibly delicate, or it can be heavier, made with thicker threads. Lace makes beautiful sheer curtains and table skirts. It has a feminine, delicate look.

LEATHER is an animal skin that has been tanned. Though not technically a fabric, it can be used to upholster anything from sofas to screens. The process of making leather involves curing, then tanning the animal hide, which softens and preserves it. Leather can also be used as a wall and floor covering, as well as to cover desktops and for bookbinding. It can be embossed and painted. A leather chair is synonymous with a traditional library. Upholstered leather furniture is often finished with a nail head trim. With leather, you would not use gimp, which is a braided trimming used as an alternative to a nail head trim, because they are two very different looks. Upholstered leather can be tufted or buttoned.

MOHAIR is a woven fabric made from the hair of the angora goat. The word mohair is thought to be derived from the Arabic word *mukhayyar,* meaning "chosen." The fiber from the angora goat has been used by people for thousands of years. Mohair is often combined with cotton or linen and is thick and durable and can be expected to wear well. Mohair is plush and dyes easily to deep colors. It is used for upholstery on sofas and chair seats and can be dressed up or dressed down. Mohair velvet was used on old movie theater seats.

MOIRÉ is a watered effect created by pressing fabric through heated rollers making a wavelike pattern. It has a formal and rather fancy look. Moiré is most often on silk, but can also be on cotton or rayon. Fabric with the moiré effect is used for upholstery or for lined curtains as well as for soft goods such as pillows and table skirts.

MUSLIN is a very basic cotton fabric with a plain weave that is sometimes printed or dyed. The name comes from Mosul, a town in northern Iraq where the fabric was originally made. Muslin has a simple, clean look. It is what upholsterers put under the primary fabric of a chair or sofa to contain the filling. Muslin is lightweight and can be used for slipcovers and soft goods such as a bedspread, bedskirt, throw pillow, or table skirt. Simple muslin curtains or a window shade suit a country house or a pared-down setting very well.

PAISLEY is a design of swirling and colorful abstract shapes. It is believed to have originated centuries ago in northern India from the tree of life motif. The design was exported and eventually reproduced outside India. The name paisley comes from a city in the southwest of Scotland where weavers made woolen shawls called paisleys, with the distinctive pattern woven into them. The paisley design can be printed on or woven into a fabric and is seen in many color combinations. Brightly colored paisley was particularly popular in the psychedelic 1960s and '70s. The paisley design adds a great pattern and color to a room.

PALAMPORES are hand-painted or printed panels of fabric often with the tree of life motif. They came from India and the name palampore is thought to be an English twist on the Hindi word *pa langposh,* meaning "bed cover." They became popular in England and Europe in the seventeenth and eighteenth centuries. The palampore is thought to be the precursor to chintz, with its floral prints. The design and colors of palampores are exquisite, and the scale of the design is large. In general, a large-scale print should be reserved for curtains of a certain size, wall hangings, or bedspreads—places with one flat plane where the whole pattern can be seen. The pattern will be lost if the fabric is used on smaller items. Antique palampores make wonderful wall hangings.

SATIN is one of the basic weaves and produces a fabric that is smooth and glossy on one side and dull on the other. Satin is typically made with silk and was first developed in China centuries ago. It is also made with cotton, linen, or synthetic yarns, which run across the width of the fabric to make it stronger. The filling yarn skips up to ten or more warp yarns, which run the length of the fabric, thus creating a smooth appearance. The shine gives satin an opulent, fancy look. It can be used in a formal situation for curtains, upholstery, and throw pillows, but it is not particularly strong. Satin is suitable for upholstery and for curtains, but you wouldn't use it where it will get a lot of wear and tear. Sateen, which is glossy like satin and constructed with a similar weave, is made of cotton. Sateen is often used as a lining material for curtains. Besides the satin weave, the other basic fabric weaves are taffeta and twill.

TAFFETA is a basic weave of fabric where each filling yarn passes alternately under and over each of the warp yarns, which run the length of the fabric, producing a crisp simple weave. Taffeta is often made with silk and has a lustrous texture. The name taffeta is derived from the Persian word *taftah*, meaning "to twist" or "woven." One thinks of taffeta for evening dresses or the taffeta bows on little girls' dresses. It is a luxurious fabric with a certain stiffness that can drape beautifully. Taffeta is used for both lined and unlined curtains, table skirts, and throw pillows. Besides taffeta, the other basic fabric weaves are twill and satin.

TAPESTRY has a ribbed surface with a design, often pictorial, that is used for wall hangings or as an upholstery fabric. Technically, tapestry is hand-woven, but today there are machine-made tapestries, which are very useful for upholstery. Centuries ago, tapestries were one of the only alternatives, besides a mural, to decorating a wall. In drafty medieval castles, they were both decorative and helped with insulation. In the fourteenth century, tapestries were made in Arras, French Flanders, and later in Tournai, Belgium. Gobelins, Beauvais, and Aubusson were ateliers in France that produced many tapestries in the seventeenth and eighteenth centuries. Tapestry fabric is durable, tough, and stylish. It has a heavy look. The scale of the design in today's machine-made tapestry is much smaller than the big handmade pictorial tapestries so popular in the past. Tapestry fabric can be used widely. It is great on upholstery such as sofas as well as on smaller pieces and throw pillows.

TOILES are cotton or linen fabrics often with bucolic scenes, figures, and landscapes printed on them. Toile was first made in India and imported to France in the late seventeenth century; those prints were called Toiles d'Indy. In the late eighteenth century, a Bavarian, Christophe-Philippe Oberkampf, started manufacturing toiles in Jouy, a town near Versailles, that were similar to the Indian prints. Toile de Jouy became instantly popular, and those prints are still reproduced widely today. Toile prints are most often executed in basic colors such as black, green, blue, deep yellow, and red on a white or off-white ground. Some of the prints record historic events, such as the discovery of Pompeii. In the 1920s a toile was printed featuring Charles Lindbergh and his first solo flight from New York to Paris.

Toile has a cozy, old-fashioned, French country look and can be used for everything from wall covering to upholstery to curtains, to bedskirts and tablecloths. It lends itself to smaller rooms and is particularly great in a bedroom with eaves and sloping walls. An entire bedroom can be covered with a toile print from wallpaper to pillow shams and upholstery for a very cozy, stylish look.

TWILL is a basic fabric weave where the filling yarn that runs the width of the fabric goes over and under two or more warp yarns that run the length of the fabric. This creates a diagonal pattern. Twill fabric can also have a herringbone pattern. Any fiber can be used for a twill weave. Denim is a particularly common twill weave. A twill weave is soft and durable. The other basic fabric weaves are taffeta and satin.

VELVET has a soft pile on one side created by loops in the warp yarns, which run the length of the fabric. Velvet can be made from silk, cotton, rayon, linen, and mohair, among other fibers. It can have crushed pile or be embossed. It can have stripes or a pattern. Silk velvet is very precious, dressy, luxurious, and a bit fragile. It can be used for upholstery or even as the fabric on a stretched lampshade. Linen velvet has a ribbed texture, is less expensive than silk velvet, and is a good all around choice that you can dress up or dress down. Cotton velvet doesn't look particularly dressy and is not as distinctive as silk or linen velvet. Mohair velvet is known to be durable and was used on old movie theater seats. All types of velvet are great for use on upholstery, curtains, table skirts, and throw pillows. Velvet has a luxurious look with rich colors. There's nothing more luxurious than chocolate-brown silk velvet!

Natural Fibers

COTTON comes from the white fluffy fibers inside the cotton boll, which is the pod also containing the seeds of the cotton plant. The word cotton comes from the Arabic *qutun*. The ancient Egyptians were known to have worn cotton as early as 2500 BC, and there is evidence that cotton was grown in India before that. When Eli Whitney invented the cotton gin in 1793, the process of separating the plant seeds from the fiber was made about fifty times faster, and the production of cotton became a big industry. Cotton is the most widely used textile fiber today; it is lightweight, easy to wash, and used to make everything from jeans to the best chintz prints.

LINEN is made from the fibers of the flax plant and has been produced for thousands of years. When the tombs of Egyptian pharaohs were opened, explorers found the mummies wrapped in linen that was in remarkably good shape. To make linen, the flax plant is pulled from the ground and taken through a multistep process to extract the fiber from the rest of the plant material. The flax seeds are used to make linseed oil, which is used in paints and linoleum, among other things. Linen holds dye well and gets softer with washing.

SILK, made from the cocoons of the silkworm, was first cultivated in China between 3000 and 2500 BC, and for more than a thousand years the Chinese kept its production a tightly guarded secret. Around 300 AD silk was first produced in India, then in about 550 AD two monks are said to have brought silkworm eggs to Byzantine Emperor Justinian's court, subsequently establishing the silk trade in the Middle East.

Sericulture is the name for the production of cultivated silk, which begins with the hatching of a silkworm. The worm eats mulberry leaves until it matures and begins to spin a cocoon for metamorphosis. The cocoons are heated to kill the worms and stop the metamorphosis process. They are then soaked in near-boiling water to loosen the filament. Once loose, the filament is wound onto a spool and twisted with other filaments to make a silk yarn. One filament can be up to nearly a half-mile long. Raw silk has not been processed to remove the coating of sericin, which is a naturally occurring compound protecting the silk filament. Raw silk has a rougher texture than silk that has been processed. All silk, however, has a lustrous texture and can be dyed rich and beautiful colors. It is used to make the finest textiles from velvet to brocade to taffeta and also fabrics for everyday use such as long underwear.

WOOL is technically the hair from sheep, camel, angora goat (called mohair), llama, alpaca, or Kashmir goat; but the word wool is usually understood to mean fiber from sheep. Sheep have been bred for their wool for thousands of years. After sheep are shorn, the wool is washed to remove wool grease, also known as lanolin, which is used in cosmetic products, and suint, which is the dried sheep sweat. The wool is then spun into thread. Wool is naturally flame-retardant, warm, and absorbent so it can be beautifully dyed. Many rugs and upholstery fabrics are made with wool as it has great warmth and texture. Wool ages well, and indeed antique wool rugs are thought to improve with time.

Synthetic Fibers

ACETATE is made from cellulose, which is the primary building block of plants. In 1905 the Swiss brothers Camille and Henri Dreyfus developed a commercial process to make cellulose acetate, which was used in celluloid plastics and for movie film. About ten years later, acetate was developed into a fiber that could be used to make textiles; it was developed shortly after rayon, which was the first synthetic fiber to be produced. In the mid-1920s acetate was first produced in the United States by the Celanese Corporation. Acetate fibers dye well, blend easily with other fibers, and drape well. The fiber can be made to be very soft or to have a crisp feel.

ACRYLIC is a versatile group of synthetic fibers made from a polymer of acrylonitrile and one or more other components. Acrylic was first mass-produced in 1950 by E. I. du Pont de Nemours and Company. It is resistant to stains, mildew, and fungus, as well as wrinkles. It is easily blended with other fibers and is used in a wide variety of textiles.

NYLON is a widely used synthetic fiber that was first commercially produced in 1939 by E. I. du Pont de Nemours and Company. It is a very strong fiber that resists shrinking, which is why it works so well for women's stockings and bathing suits. It also is widely used for household textiles, often blended with other fibers. Many wall-to-wall carpets are made with nylon. A consideration with nylon is that it does not hold up to prolonged exposure to direct sunlight.

POLYESTER is a fiber made from mixing alcohols and carboxyl acids. First produced in the United States in the early 1950s by E. I. du Pont de Nemours and Company, polyester doesn't wrinkle, is inexpensive, and is stronger than natural fibers. Cotton, wool, and rayon are often blended with polyester in fabrics for household use. Polyester can sometimes have a sheen, but doesn't always. There are many attractive fabrics with a polyester content, which is something to consider in rooms that will get a lot of wear and tear.

RAYON is made from cellulose, which is the primary building block of plants. Produced in 1910 by the American Viscose Company, it was the first synthetic fiber made. There are a number of types of rayon, but the most common is viscose rayon. To make viscose rayon, wood chips are treated until they turn into a thick liquid, which is then formed into fibers. Rayon is extremely versatile and can be made to feel like cotton, silk, wool, or linen. It drapes well, and is very absorbent so it dyes well. It is often blended with cotton, linen, or wool. It shrinks and stretches sometimes more than cotton does, so fabrics with rayon should be dry cleaned unless they have been specifically treated to withstand laundering.

floors and
floor coverings

3

When deciding what to do with a floor, consider two issues: the floor itself and the carpeting or rug that covers it. Budget, the look, and how you plan to use the space will help you decide what to do. A solid wood floor is timeless and beautiful, but if it's in bad condition, it should be refinished or covered with wall-to-wall carpeting. Floors such as concrete, stone, and ceramic tile are durable but hard on the feet in spaces where people stand a lot. Resilient floors such as vinyl, linoleum, cork, or rubber have some give and so are easier on the feet. Wall-to-wall carpeting is softer on the feet and can make a room look larger. It also absorbs sound. Area rugs are an investment that can easily be brought to your next house. ■ It's important to check with manufacturers, distributors, or installers about which sealers and which cleaning products to use on floors. It is most practical to do all work to the floors before you move into a space. When renovating or moving, protect the floors.

Carpeting

Carpeting can have a low pile (about a quarter-of-an-inch thick) or a high pile (which is usually a half-inch or more) — up to two or three inches for shag carpeting popular in the 1970s. Both low pile and high pile can be loop (the strands of yarn are in loops) or cut (the strands are cut). Low loop pile is often used for commercial and high traffic areas, as it tends to be sturdier and will not show footprints and shading as much as cut pile. Cut pile tends to have a softer look and is used in less trafficked spaces.

Spaces appear larger with **wall-to-wall** carpeting, and it is a great option if you don't want to refinish the floor underneath. It also helps to keep sound levels down. Most carpeting made for wall-to-wall installation can also be made into an area rug if the borders are bound, which many carpet distributors can do. This can be an economical way to get an area rug for a larger space.

There are three ways to install wall-to-wall carpeting: padding and tackless, in which a thin strip of wood with sharp tacks is nailed down around the perimeter of the room, then a layer of padding is put down, and the carpet is laid over the padding and secured by the tacks; glue-down is when the carpet is glued directly to the floor; and double-stick, in which padding is glued directly to the floor and the carpet is glued to the padding. For residential purposes, padding and tackless is most widely used. Glue-down is most often used in commercial spaces and in rooms below grade, or ground level. Double-stick is also most often used for commercial installation.

Carpeting, as well as rugs, can be either woven or tufted. Woven is the older technique, in which rugs are made on a loom, and the pile and the backing are created together, at the same time. Tufted carpets can be made faster than woven carpets through a process whereby the yarn is punched through an existing backing.

The words "carpeting" and "rug" are often used interchangeably. Traditionally, carpeting means for wall-to-wall installation, and a rug is bound and loose. While the distinction between carpeting and area rugs, such as Oriental rugs, is not black and white, they do fall into separate categories.

AXMINSTER is a type of carpet weave. In 1755 a man named Thomas Whitty established a carpet factory in the town of Axminster, England. Well-known architects of the time, such as the Scottish Neoclassicist Robert Adam (1728–1792), had Axminster area rugs custom-made for some of the finest and grandest houses. Today the Axminster weave, which uses stiff warp fibers, is still commonly used in woven carpets. Axminster carpets are made in a wide variety of patterns and use a large number of colors. A practical consideration is that Axminster carpets only bend in one direction due to the stiff warp. This is something to double-check if you plan to install carpet on stairs: make sure the carpet can run in the direction you want. Preferably Axminster should be installed with padding and tackless. It is possible to glue down Axminster, but it's not recommended (as the glue can seep through the backing).

BERBER is a carpet made with a natural-colored speckled, or heathered, yarn. It can have a cut or loop pile, but it is most commonly associated with a low loop. These carpets have a natural look and a rich texture that do well in an informal room. It can be used as a neutral, unifying floor covering throughout a house—from room to room—and can look great with area rugs over it. Berber carpeting can either be woven, which is the traditional way of making rugs, or tufted, which is a relatively modern method of construction.

BROADLOOM CARPET refers to the width of the loom and therefore the width of the carpet. Standard broadloom widths are 12 feet; 13 feet, 2 inches; or 15 feet, which means fewer seams than if you used carpeting from a narrow loom. Minimal seams are preferable. Narrow loom carpets come in standard widths of 2 feet, 3 inches and 3 feet. It is more labor intensive to install them as there are more seams to sew together. There are some beautiful narrow loom carpets, though, so you just have to weigh the pros and cons.

COCOA MAT is doormat material made from natural bristle on a rubber base. It is cut to size and glued down, usually near a front door or back door. It is very practical for country houses and high-traffic areas, as the coarse bristles scrape dirt off shoes. An entire floor of a mudroom in a country house can be covered in cocoa mat, which, with a wooden bench and some hooks on the wall for coats, will have a cozy country look and keep the mess out of the house.

SISAL is a natural fiber used to make flat, woven floor covering; the term sisal has come to include carpeting also made with jute, seagrass, and other natural materials. Sisal has a rough texture and a natural color that ranges from pale to dark; it can also be dyed. Sisal can be installed wall-to-wall or bound as an area rug. It is widely available and works very well with a number of looks, from Asian to country to urban. It is used often in contemporary design. Wall-to-wall sisal is a great way to cover up a floor that you don't want to refinish; it works well with rugs such as kilims over it. Some sisal can be rough on bare feet, so it's not ideal for bathrooms or bedrooms. There is also wool sisal — wool woven to look like sisal — which is softer but has basically the same look.

Sisal can be installed either with padding and tackless or glued-down. With padding and tackless there is more resiliency and, most likely, a neater edge at the wall. The best way to install wall-to-wall sisal, especially if you are using padding and tackless, is to have the rug delivered and spread out for a day before securing it down. Since sisal is made from natural materials, it will shrink or expand depending on the humidity. Giving the rug a day to acclimatize to its new home will minimize any buckling after it is installed. If you glue down sisal, it's a good idea to put quarter-round shoe molding (page 32) down along the baseboards to cover any imperfect edges at the wall.

TUFTED CARPETS are an alternative to woven carpets such as Axminster and Wilton. They can be made faster than woven carpets and are generally less expensive. This relatively modern way to make a carpet was first seen in the twentieth century. Tufting machines punch the yarn through an existing backing of jute or synthetic material. The backing is coated in latex and then a secondary backing is applied with more latex. Tufted carpets can be loop or cut pile. In high-traffic areas, tufted carpets can be glued down as the backing will protect the rug fibers from the glue. A tufted carpet can also be installed using padding and tackless. In a commercial or high-traffic space, you can use either a tufted or a woven carpet; however, a woven carpet should have a backing that makes it suitable for glue-down installation.

VELVET CARPET refers to the texture, which is a smooth cut pile usually with a low profile. It can be tufted or woven and is often a solid color. While some carpets are better quality than others, velvet carpeting has a luxurious, soft look and is suitable to low-traffic areas. You would not put it in a busy hallway (as the traffic pattern will be noticeable in time).

WILTON is a type of weave with pile on the front, and the yarns run along the back of the carpet. It is made using a jacquard attachment and can have intricate patterns and a variety of colors. The pile and the backing are woven at the same time. A Wilton carpet, named after the town in England where the factory producing carpets of this weave was built in 1655, can have either cut or loop pile. Like Axminster carpets, Wiltons are generally more expensive than tufted carpeting as they take longer to make. Unlike the Axminster, though, Wilton bends in both directions and so can be installed in any direction on a staircase. The backing on a Wilton carpet is open, so it should be installed using padding and tackless, not glue-down, as the glue can seep into the fibers.

Carpet Installation

Carpet installation requires deciding what direction to run the carpet. There are no hard and fast rules. A general guideline is if the carpet is a solid color or has a geometric design with no particular direction, lay the carpet with the least number of visible seams. This will depend on your furniture layout. In a bedroom you might just have one seam running the length of the room and under the bed.

DOUBLE-STICK INSTALLATION is used mostly in commercial spaces. Padding is glued to the floor and carpet is glued to the padding. In residential design this method is rarely used because gluing the pad directly onto a wood or finished floor can damage the floor. Padding and tackless, which uses no glue, provides the same resiliency.

GLUE-DOWN is when the carpet is glued directly onto the floor, with no pad underneath. It is used more often in commercial design, in basements, or areas below ground level, or grade, where there's a danger of leaks or floods. It's not as resilient as padding and tackless, an alternative type of installation, and will be harder on the feet. Woven carpets with open backs, such as Wiltons and Axminsters, are best installed using padding and tackless and not glue-down as the glue can seep into the fibers of the rug.

PADDING AND TACKLESS is when a thin strip of wood with sharp tacks is nailed down around the perimeter of the room, then a layer of padding is put down, and the carpet is laid over the padding and secured by the tacks. This method is used mostly for residential design. The padding increases the carpet's resilience. For carpets with an open weave, such as Axminster and Wilton, is it best to use padding and tackless.

STAIR RODS are metal rods—often brass—that are placed across a step where the tread (the horizontal part of the step) meets the riser (the vertical part). They used to serve the practical purpose of holding the carpet in place on a flight of stairs, but today they are decorative. Used widely with many different styles, stair rods add a touch of formality and a nice detail. Carpeting with stair rods should have a waterfall installation.

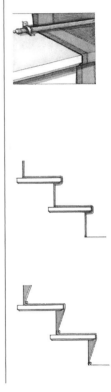

UPHOLSTERED INSTALLATION is one of two ways to install carpeting on steps. The carpet is firmly secured to the underside of the nosing of the step and to the riser. The alternative to upholstered installation is waterfall. Upholstered installation has a more tailored look, while waterfall has a more traditional look.

In **WATERFALL INSTALLATION** the carpet falls over the nosing of the tread and is secured below to where the horizontal tread and the vertical riser meet. Unlike in upholstered installation, the carpeting is not secured to the underside of the nosing or the riser.

Ceramic Floor Tiles

Ceramic floor tiles have been around for thousands of years and are still widely used today. Ancient Chinese and Roman civilizations both used ceramic tiles. In Greek temples, churches, and mosques, early tilework on floors and walls was often stunningly beautiful and varied. Today, ceramic tiles can be used in any room of the house. Because of their strength and easy maintenance, they are often used in kitchens and bathrooms.

In a pared-down contemporary setting, ceramic floor tiles are likely to be consistent in color and shape. In traditional styles — from Spanish to Turkish — tiles of varying colors and shapes are used together to create pattern. The size of the tiles and the pattern should be proportional to the size of the room. It's best to save the big patterns for bigger rooms. Ceramic tiles are harder on the feet than a resilient floor covering, such as vinyl, cork, or rubber, and objects dropped on the floor are likely to break. On the other hand, a ceramic tile floor can last forever. Tiles are cool in hot climates. In cold climates tiles can get chilly — but radiant heat coils under a tile floor can help. Ceramic tiles can be set on the square or the diagonal.

TERRA-COTTA TILES are made of fired clay that has a warm and earthy reddish-brown color. In Italian, *terra cotta* means "baked earth." Terra-cotta tiles are used around the world — from Italy to Mexico. They lend themselves to a country look, a rustic look, or to a Mediterranean look, and they are widely used in Southwestern and Spanish styles. The floor tiles can be bought finished or unfinished, meaning either presealed or unsealed. The tiles have to be sealed to protect them from wear. Buying them unsealed allows for more flexibility in choosing the gloss level and type of sealer but also makes for a more labor-intensive installation. The tiles come in different sizes. The size of the tile should be proportional to the size of the room. Terra-cotta tiles are popular and for good reason. They are durable and have a wonderful, warm color. They work almost anywhere and can be used equally well in kitchens and hallways as well as in major rooms of a house. A terra-cotta tile floor lasts forever.

Concrete Floors

Concrete floors have an industrial look that has been gaining popularity in recent years. You are likely to see concrete floors in art galleries and lofts. Concrete has a pared-down look and can either be left bare or covered with area rugs. These floors can be colored a few different ways. Pigments can be added directly to the concrete, the floor can be stained, or the floor can be painted. It's best to wait 60 to 90 days for the concrete to completely cure before painting. Etching the concrete will give the paint more surface to grab onto. A concrete floor should be sealed. There

Mosaic

Mosaic is a design or figurative picture made from small pieces, or tesserae, of stone, glass, or clay. The Romans developed what we think of today as typical mosaic patterns—which were used on the floor and, later, on the walls. Byzantine  churches are filled with wonderful and colorful examples of mosaics studded with gold. And, just to prove that great ideas never disappear, mosaic has been used frequently in contemporary design.

These days, instead of creating mosaic tessera by tessera, you can buy strips with many tesserae already formed into patterns. There are traditional designs seen in places such as Pompeii, and modern treatments using one vivid color, in a bathroom, a kitchen, or a major room in the house.

are many types of sealers, and which one you choose will depend on the location and intended use.

Concrete tends to crack or flake when there is any movement in the subfloor or walls; therefore, it is a good idea to cut joints into the floor to ease pressure and prevent cracking and flaking, especially around doorways and other pressure points. Concrete is harder on the feet than a more resilient floor covering, such as vinyl tiles or cork, and anything you drop on it is likely to break. A poured concrete floor is heavy and some buildings may not be able to bear the weight—this is something to consult an architect or builder on before you call in the concrete mixer.

Laminate Flooring

Laminate flooring has multiple layers including a digital image—of wood or stone for example—with a thick protective layer over it and a solid backing under it. It looks like wood or stone but is mostly synthetic. Laminate floors have been used for longer in Europe than in the United States. A laminate floor is relatively easy to install; it can either be glued down or "float," which means that the strips of flooring lock into each other and don't need to be affixed to the floor. It can be placed over some existing floor treatments, which is a plus if you're on a tight budget as it means not necessarily having to rip up the existing floor. Laminate floors cannot be refinished, but if a section is damaged it can be replaced. Like many floor coverings, laminate can scratch and should be vacuumed and damp-mopped regularly.

Leather Floor Tiles

Leather floor tiles come in a variety of colors and sizes. They can be very chic and work well to muffle sound. They are soft on the feet and have a luxurious texture. Leather changes over time as a patina forms. Wear will show and the tiles will not stay pristine. Leather is not the most economical floor covering, but it can be beautiful. It is well suited to a library that is either traditional or more contemporary. It's best not to use leather tiles in very dry climates or in rooms with a lot of moisture. Leather needs to be waxed a couple of times a year; check with manufacturers, distributors, or installers familiar with the product to find out what they recommend.

Resilient Floor Covering

Resilient floor covering is made from materials that have some give yet retain their shape. Resilient floor covering materials include cork, linoleum, rubber, and vinyl. They are softer than ceramic tiles, cement, stone, and even wood floors. This means they will be more comfortable to stand on for long periods of time. Resilient floors can also offer soundproofing and some insulation. Since they are softer, they will generally scratch more easily than harder floors and should be vacuumed and damp-mopped regularly. Resilient floors generally shrink and expand depending on the humidity and temperature. It's a good idea to allow the materials to acclimate to the room where they will be installed for a day or two before gluing them down.

CORK FLOORS are made with real cork, which comes from the bark of the cork oak tree, *Quercus suber*, found in the Mediterranean region—Portugal in particular. Cork is considered eco-friendly because the bark grows back and the tree isn't cut down. Cork is often used in eco-conscious design projects. The color of cork is warm, and the natural pattern can add an interesting design element to a room. Cork floors are known to be soft on the feet and acoustically excellent. From a kitchen to a library, a cork floor can be great. Like a solid wood floor, cork can be finished with either wax or polyurethane. With wax, the more traditional finish, the floor develops a lustrous patina over many years but also requires waxing at least once a year. A polyurethane finish is lower-maintenance and will be more durable in areas such as the kitchen. Because cork can be damaged by water, it's important to clean up spills quickly and to avoid soaking the floor when cleaning. Cork is a natural material, so it can expand and contract considerably. There are also cork tiles made with vinyl.

LINOLEUM is a natural mixture made from linseed oil, which is oxidized and mixed with powdered wood, ground limestone, resins, dyeing agents, and pigments. This mixture is affixed to a natural or synthetic backing. The recipe for linoleum was patented in 1863 by an Englishman named Frederick Walton. Quite durable, the material was widely used in both commercial and residential spaces until vinyl flooring became readily available in the late 1940s. Vinyl, a synthetic, is much easier to maintain, and it significantly diminished the linoleum market. These days, people sometimes interchange the terms "linoleum" and "vinyl sheeting," although the materials are entirely different. Linoleum comes in a variety of color choices and almost always in sheets. It's possible to create a patterned floor using different colors of linoleum that are cut out and inlaid into a sheet of linoeum. Although you rarely see such inlay work today, it is an interesting design idea. Linoleum floor covering is at its best when it's waxed regularly and stripped periodically to remove the wax build-up.

RUBBER FLOORING has been used for centuries. It was originally made from real rubber, from the sap of the South American tree *Hevea brasiliensis* that was later widely grown in Asia.

Now rubber flooring is made with synthetic and recycled rubber. Seen most often on the floors at airports and in commercial spaces, a rubber floor can also be great in a laundry room, kitchen, or playroom. Rubber floors can have an industrial look, but there are designs and colors being made specifically for residential use that have a contemporary and homey feel. It comes in a wide variety of colors with either a flat or a textured surface. It is easily washable, burn resistant, durable, slip resistant, and absorbs noise. In bathrooms and kitchens it works well because it's soft on the feet and can handle a spill. Some types of rubber will be damaged by oil, so be sure to ask about specific products.

Creating a Country Look

A country-style house can be wonderfully cozy and inviting. Whether you live in the country or the city, you can achieve a country look by focusing on warm colors throughout and furniture, floor, and window treatments made from natural materials. A country look has slightly rough edges and shows the hand of the craftsman.

Elements that lend themselves to a country look are pine furniture, black iron or oiled hardware, decorative baskets, and throw blankets on sofas and chairs. Architectural details are traditional but not overstated: a simple crown molding, baseboard, and perhaps a chair rail. Upholstered chairs and sofas are more likely to have loose seat cushions and be covered in a simple print or woven design.

Floor treatments to consider for a country look are wall-to-wall sisal carpeting with area rugs over it, wood floors with area rugs, a painted wood floor, or terra-cotta tile. Kilims and rag rugs lend themselves to a country look. Lighting can be provided by table and standing lamps, and perhaps hanging fixtures such as a carriage lantern or a simple brass, iron, or tole chandelier. Traditional wood, brass, iron, or tole wall sconces would also be suitable. A very cozy country look for a bedroom is to use the same toile print everywhere, from wallpaper to upholstery to bedspread.

VINYL FLOORING is made using a synthetic material that was invented in the 1920s by Waldo Lonsbury Semon, an American, who worked at the B.F. Goodrich Company. Semon took polyvinyl chloride, or PVC, and created a process to make it flexible and useful for applications such as flooring. Vinyl flooring was not widely marketed until the late 1940s, and it became very popular at least in part because it is very easy to maintain. It is still widely used today.

Vinyl comes in tiles and sheeting in a wide variety of colors and patterns. There are wax and no-wax varieties; no-wax floors are particularly easy to maintain. Vinyl is a good solution for kitchens, laundry rooms, and bathrooms. An attractive use of vinyl tile is to alternate two solid colors set on the square or the diagonal. A kitchen can be spruced up by having a checkerboard of black-and-white tiles, for example. Since vinyl is thin and flexible, any variations or imperfections in the floor below will eventually wear through and become visible on the vinyl surface. This makes it especially important to make sure the subfloor is level and completely clean before installation. Vinyl is usually glued down but self-adhesive tiles are also available.

Rugs

Rugs have been made throughout history in all different corners of the world. From location to location, different styles were developed, creating regional designs and textures. There are antique rugs, and there are new ones that are made using traditional patterns and motifs. An antique rug is technically at least 100 years old, although a 90-year-old rug may be considered an antique. A semi-antique rug is 40 to 70 years old and generally is not as valuable. An antique rug is an investment and the condition should be carefully examined before buying—one in good condition will increase in value over time.

Older rugs are made by hand and show irregularities that add character and originality. New rugs can also be made by hand or else by machine. Reproduction rugs are available in many different styles. Area rugs are traditionally made from wool, silk, or cotton. The terms "carpeting" and "rug" are often used interchangeably. Traditionally, carpeting refers to wall-to-wall installation, whereas a rug is bound and loose.

It's important to have a good nonslip rug pad under any area rug on a hard floor.

ANIMAL-HIDE RUGS can be very chic. They have an interesting shape and texture, either short and bristly or shaggy depending on the animal. A cowhide rug has a Western look that is often used in contemporary design and can be great in any room. There are also cowhide rugs stenciled with zebra stripes. Bearskin rugs, with a head still intact and mouth open showing big, sharp teeth, were often seen in nineteenth-century Victorian houses. Finding such a rug today requires combing flea markets and auctions, but can make quite a statement, on the floor or on the wall. A bearskin can also impart a Hemingway-esque hunting lodge look. Finally, sheepskins make wonderful throw rugs in front of the fire or by a bed.

AUBUSSON RUGS are made with a flat weave technique and are generally quite ornate. The name comes from the town of Aubusson in central France where tapestry works were established in approximately the seventeenth century or earlier. (Aubusson was also well known for producing tapestries.) These rugs often have floral designs with architectural elements and beautiful soft colors. An Aubusson rug is delicate and best used in a room that is not heavily trafficked. It has a very French and formal look to it.

BESSARABIAN RUGS are from the region of Bessarabia on the western shore of the Black Sea that has been a part of both Romania and the Ukraine—depending on the political situation. The designs are often floral with elegantly drawn motifs and colors in earth tones. The style shows both French and Oriental influences. Bessarabian rugs are almost always woven, meaning they have no pile. The rare Bessarabian rug with pile is very valuable. Bessarabian rugs are not as formal as, for example, Savonnerie or Aubusson rugs.

BRAIDED RUGS are made with braided strips of cotton or wool. The strips are sewn together making a rug that is often oval but can also be square or rectangular. Braided rugs have an informal, rustic appearance and, these days, can be either machine made or handmade. Use braided rugs, either cotton or wool, in a country house in any room. They are versatile and attractive and can also be used in an informal city setting.

FLOKATI RUGS are Greek hand-woven area rugs made from 100-percent wool that are almost always a natural, off-white color. They have been produced for centuries and were a staple of the early Greek shepherds. In the 1970s these sheep's wool rugs were very popular, and in recent years they have reemerged in contemporary design. Flokatis are very shaggy, with a pile 3 or 4 inches long. They are cozy and have a great texture. They are relatively inexpensive and not too big, which makes them easy to take with you to your next home. They are great in a bedroom or a living room or really any room that is not formal in the traditional sense. They are best used as throw rugs over a wood floor or over a flat floor covering such as sisal. Flokatis suit any look from contemporary to Mediterranean.

KILIMS are hand-knotted rugs that are thin, lightweight and durable. *Kilim* is a Turkish word that implies the flat weave technique. Kilims typically have a geometric design that can be bold and colorful. They are used in a wide variety of looks—from country to contemporary—and create a great splash of color on floors of wood, terra-cotta tile, or sisal. Kilims are often in Southwestern style. They can also be used as wall hangings. Over time the colors of a kilim fade to beautiful soft hues.

NEEDLEPOINT RUGS are made with wool yarn that is cross-stitched onto a heavy canvas backing. Any variation of color and pattern is possible. Needlepoint rugs primarily come from France, England, and, to a lesser extent, Portugal. They can have fine or large stitching. The large stitching is called gros-pointe; the smaller stitch is petit-pointe. Needlepoint rugs are still made today, but if you find an antique one in good condition, it will be a jewel. They are versatile and can be used from living room to bedroom. The design of the needlepoint will have much to do with the look of the rug. Besides rugs, needlepoint can also be used for upholstery and for throw pillows.

ORIENTAL RUG is a general term for rugs that are Caucasian, Chinese, Indian, Persian, and Turkish. These rugs are named after the place where they were made or the people who made them. All have unique traditional designs. Many have a center medallion in the design, but others have an all-over pattern without a medallion. The richness of color and the intrinsic design value make them works of art for the floor. Oriental rugs suit both contemporary and traditional design. They are timeless and highly versatile. An Oriental rug is a purchase that you will have forever. Here are the major types of Oriental rugs:

Caucasian Rugs come from the region between northwest Iran and eastern Turkey including Armenia and Azerbaijan. Of these rugs, there are three main types: Karabakh, Kazak, and Shirvan rugs. Others types of Caucasian rugs include Daghestan, Kuba, Shendje, and Soumak. Although there certainly are some Caucasian rugs that are more refined, they generally have primary colors and a provincial look.

Chinese Rugs dating from early times are sometimes called Nangxia after the region where they were made. Basically all traditional Chinese rugs have Buddhist or Taoist motifs including the endless knot and the dragon. The predominant colors in Chinese rugs are navy blue, ivory, and yellow. A Chinese rug will almost always have blue in it. They are made with silk and wool piles and often have a pale background with a more deeply colored design.

Indian Rugs are often from Agra and Amritsar. Other types of Indian rugs include Kashmir, Lahore, and Srinagar. Most Indian rugs have softer colors and a less rigid design than other Oriental rugs. The designs are similar to Persian rugs but tend to be less opulent.

Persian Rugs come from the area that is now Iran. They include the popular Tabriz, Heriz, and Sultanabad rugs. Tabriz rugs, which come from a town in northwest Iran, have a more formal look than some other Persian rugs. Heriz rugs tend to have geometric patterns and colors in jewel tones, meaning deep reds and blues. Sultanabad rugs come from the Arak region in northwest Iran and have a short pile. Other types of Persian rugs are Bakhtiary, Bijar, Feraghan, Kerman, Sarook, Senneh, and Serapi rugs.

Turkish Rugs come mainly from central Turkey and include Anatolian, Hereke, and

Oushak rugs. Oushak rugs are quite popular and for good reason. The designs are fairly informal and larger in scale. In general they are attractive and highly versatile.

PAINTED FLOOR CLOTHS are literally paintings that go on the floor. Heavy canvas is stretched and painted, often using stencils, and coated with a protective finish. Floor cloths were first popular in early eighteenth-century England and America. It is possible to buy pre-primed canvas for this purpose at art supply stores. If you're preparing the canvas yourself, which you might do for a floor cloth that is not a standard size, the canvas must be stretched first and both sides of it primed before painting. It's important to talk to an expert at an art supply store about which products to use. Painted floor cloths offer a great opportunity to have a custom-made floor treatment with the right scale, colors, and pattern for the room.

RAG RUGS are traditionally made using scraps of cotton and wool textiles. Rag rugs were born of necessity on the American prairie in the late nineteenth century, out of clothes worn thin from hard work. They are generally not very big and often are round or oval. During the Arts and Crafts Movement at the start of the twentieth century, these rugs were particularly popular. They are made by pulling scraps of cloth through burlap with a hook or with braided strips of fabric sewn together. They tend to have simple designs. Rag rugs can be used in a country house, a beach house, a child's room, or by a bed. They have a cozy handmade feel. They go very well with the light and airy Scandinavian or Swedish style.

SAVONNERIE RUGS were first made in France and graced the grand estates of nobility in the seventeenth and eighteenth centuries. The Savonnerie rug factory was established in the early seventeenth century in an old soap factory, thus the name, which means "soap factory" in French. A Savonnerie rug, which has a thick pile, is best used in a special room without a lot of traffic. They are formal and have a very European look. The style has been widely reproduced and Savonnerie-style rugs come from all over the world.

TIBETAN RUGS, with a luxuriously thick pile, are mostly handmade in Nepal for export to the West. Tibetan rugs are made with wool or silk pile or a combination. The motifs are sometimes traditional Tibetan Buddhist images, but many of the rugs are made in solid colors and with contemporary designs to meet the demands of the Western market. Their rich simplicity makes them suitable for almost any style. The colors are generally very beautiful. Tibetan rugs have become widely available and more popular in recent years. They are generally high-quality rugs that are a good value.

Stone Floors

Stone floors add a natural element to a room and have wonderful texture and variety of color. Stone is durable and, as many historic buildings show, it can last for centuries. It has an architectural look that can be either traditional or contemporary depending on the stone, the finish, and the setting. The colors and quality of stone will vary from quarry to quarry. Even within specific quarries, the stone will vary from area to area. Stone can either have a matte or polished finish. Matte is generally more versatile; polished has a dressier look. Stone can also have a "flamed" finish, where the surface is rough and has a rustic look.

Stone can be installed in slabs or as tile—slabs are much larger and thicker than tile. Stone floors, like ceramic tiles, are hard on the feet and can be cold to the touch. In colder climates, radiant heat in the floor can be a good way to keep it from being chilly. Objects dropped on a stone floor are likely to break. Also, it is important to check how to seal stone. This will vary depending on the type of stone and its intended use. Besides floors, stone can also be used in many other places around a house: on walls, countertops, backsplashes, mantelpieces, fireplace hearth and facing, windowsills, and thresholds, to name a few.

FLAGSTONES are flat, gray, often irregularly shaped paving stones that are used in both exteriors and interiors. They are often made of sandstone or slate and have a rustic look. Flagstones are typically used as flooring on a patio or a terrace, in greenhouses, or anywhere from an entrance hall to a mudroom.

GRANITE is hard and durable. It is an igneous rock, meaning it is produced deep inside the earth under tremendous heat and pressure and is composed mostly of the minerals feldspar, mica, and quartz. The colors of granite can vary widely from a light gray to pink to a dark charcoal color depending on the mineral content. Granite is frequently used in contemporary design. A granite tile floor in a kitchen can be attractive. Granite is also frequently used for countertops in the kitchen.

LIMESTONE typically has a warm neutral color but can also come in red or green tints. It is a sedimentary rock that is composed mostly of calcium carbonate and shows interesting irregularities. You can often see the fossils of plants and small animals embedded in it. Limestone is porous and not as hard as granite, but for average residential use, this shouldn't make a difference. It can be polished but is more frequently seen with a matte finish. Limestone has a timeless look that can be used with a wide variety of styles.

MARBLE is the Rolls-Royce of stone. In Classical architecture, marble was ubiquitous. Marble is limestone that has been essentially cooked in the earth under great pressure; it is a metamorphic rock. It comes in many colors, from white to neutral to yellow to green to pink to black. Installing marble in alternating black and white squares on the floor is an age-old design. You're likely to see that pattern in a grand entrance or a lobby. It can be polished to a high shine or honed to a matte finish.

SLATE typically has a blue-gray color but also comes in other colors—from yellow to purple. It is fine-grained and splits easily on parallel planes. Slate is shale that has been heated and compressed in the earth. It is frequently used for roof tiles and fireplace facing in addition to floor tiles. Flagstones, used for paving, are often made from slate. It has a rustic look.

TRAVERTINE has a neutral color with a yellowish to pinkish tint. The surface of travertine has irregularities that add an interesting texture, and the pale color reflects light. It is a sedimentary stone composed mainly of calcite and is mostly found in Italy. The irregularities in travertine can be filled if you want a smoother surface. It has a warm and natural appearance that is well suited to many different looks, from contemporary to traditional. Travertine is often seen on walls as well as floors. It can be used throughout a house, from kitchens to living rooms.

Wood Floors

Wood floors are timeless. Hardwood refers to a broad category of deciduous trees: oak, ash, cherry, maple, poplar, and walnut. Pine is not technically a hardwood but is still used successfully for flooring, but it will dent more easily than woods such as oak. Wood floors can either be solid wood or have a veneer of wood affixed to a lesser surface. The traditional floor is solid wood, which can be refinished many times and therefore will last for decades or even generations. Floors with veneers of wood are generally too thin to be sanded and therefore cannot be refinished—or only a few times. The ability to sand and refinish a floor means your investment will last longer and provide more flexibility and versatility down the road.

Solid wood floors are typically three-quarters of an inch thick and add to the value of a house. Oak and maple are commonly used for floors today. Solid wood should not be used in areas with high moisture—such as below ground level. The wood comes either pre-finished, which makes installation easier, or unfinished, which allows more flexibility and control over the final color.

Traditionally, solid wood floors had a wax finish requiring regular maintenance. Today, wood floors are often finished with polyurethane, which only requires damp-mopping as needed. A wax-finished floor that is well maintained has a beautiful luster, but a low-maintenance polyurethane finish is more in keeping with today's busy lifestyles. A flat or eggshell polyurethane finish most closely resembles the old-fashioned wax finish. In a more contemporary setting you might have a glossier wood floor. It is well worth the investment to restore an existing solid wood floor if it's in bad condition; restoring entails sanding, staining, and either waxing or varnishing with polyurethane.

Engineered wood looks much like solid wood once it's installed. It is constructed with multiple layers, like plywood, and is topped with a veneer. Engineered wood will not warp or expand and contract like solid wood does, and therefore can be used below ground—as in basements or sunken rooms. It depends on the product, but it is sometimes possible to refinish engineered wood a couple of times. Laminate floor covering can simulate the look of wood but is a laminated image that cannot be refinished.

BAMBOO FLOORING resembles a wood floor, though bamboo is technically a grass and not a wood. Bamboo is environmentally friendly because it grows quickly. Much bamboo comes from China. The boards, made of layers of bamboo, are relatively hard and stable. It can be sanded a few times—though it's important to check from manufacturer to manufacturer. Bamboo is not a traditional material for floors, but its light, natural look is well suited to contemporary design.

Wood Floor Patterns

HERRINGBONE, a traditional pattern for a solid wood floor, adds interesting detail. Boards are laid in a zigzag, also called a chevron. It is suitable for formal settings and is frequently seen in older houses and apartments. You sometimes see a herringbone patterned floor with two colors of stain, or two different types of wood, so the pattern has alternating colors. For a finished look, a patterned wood floor should be framed by a border of cross-banding running parallel to the walls. Brick and tile can also be laid in a herringbone pattern.

PARQUET is an inlaid wood floor in which strips of wood create geometric patterns. Parquet flooring was first seen in seventeenth-century Europe. A well-known design is Parquet de Versailles, a pattern used in the Hall of Mirrors at Versailles, among other places. There is nothing more beautiful than a solid wood parquet floor, but it is not common today as it's quite expensive. Much parquet flooring today is a veneer. A downside to veneered flooring is that it is generally not thick enough to sand, which means it can't be refinished. However, with some brands it is possible to sand the floor up to a few times.

Decorative Treatments for Wood Floors

Wood floors can be stained, painted, or bleached. They can be a solid color or patterned. A wood floor in good condition lends itself to staining as the wood grain will show through. Staining will not conceal imperfections in the floor as painting does. Wood stain colors range from light to ebony. A light wood floor is very suitable in a beach house, a contemporary setting, or a Swedish look. A dark wood floor is more urban and traditional. Most commonly seen and most versatile is a medium brown stain. The lightest wood floors are bleached.

It is possible, and can be very beautiful, to create geometric patterns using different stains. A herringbone wood floor will sometimes alternate boards that are stained and bleached, which can look great. Unlike a painted floor, stain will not crack or chip.

If you have an inferior wood floor, it's very clever to paint it. A painted wood floor will crack and chip over time—it should be expected. It can look great and age more gracefully if it's antiqued, or distressed, to begin with. Antiquing involves applying a coat or two of glaze and sanding. Painted wood floors are very suitable for Swedish and country looks.

PLANK WOOD FLOORS have a more rustic look than herringbone, parquet, or strip wood floors. The boards are at least 3 inches wide and are uniform in width. A **random-width plank** floor, illustrated here, is made with planks that vary in width and length; this also has a rustic look. In eighteenth- and nineteenth-century America, and even earlier, pine plank floors were typical. Older planks are wider—up to 16 inches or more—than new planks found today. Antique and salvage stores sell old pine planks that are quite beautiful and have a country look. Old pine often turns a deeper, richer color over time.

STRIP WOOD FLOORS have boards that are less than 3 inches wide and are all a uniform width. The boards run in the same direction. A strip wood floor is a classic hardwood floor. Its styles are varied, from traditional to contemporary. It is not rustic like a wide plank floor. The look of the floor is mostly determined by how it is finished. A glossy polyurethane finish tends to have a more contemporary look, while a flatter finish will more closely resemble a traditional wax finish. A medium brown color is traditional, whereas a lighter color can have a more contemporary look or be suited to a beach house, hot climate, or Swedish look.

Creating a Mediterranean Look

The Mediterranean look is light and airy. It creates an al fresco feeling of the indoors meeting the outdoors. Mediterranean architecture tends to have thick walls covered in lime wash or stucco. While the complete architectural style might be difficult to reproduce outside the Mediterranean region, the essence of the look can be recreated basically anywhere—from country to city.

Elements of a Mediterranean look include wood-beamed ceilings, ceramic tiles, iron hardware, and natural fabrics such as rough-hewn linens and medium- to heavyweight cottons. The walls are white with splashes of color from a seat cushion, a throw pillow, or a rug.

The floor might be stone or ceramic tiles—such as terracotta—with a flokati or sisal area rug. Louvered shutters or woven wood shades are appropriate window treatments. The look is uncluttered and pared down.

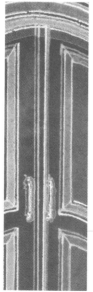

furniture

4

Furniture is key to the decoration of a house. The style of furniture generally blends with and complements the architectural style. When starting a project, it's best to begin by focusing on the basics: a good bed, a comfortable place to read and relax, and a table and chairs to sit at for meals. These basics are readily available from both commercial and custom sources. Also, searching attics, auctions, and flea markets can turn up some treasures, which with a little retouching, reupholstering, or simply a good dusting can be favorites for years to come. For smaller spaces, think about how a single piece of furniture can serve multiple functions. A drop-leaf table in a living room—or even a front hall—can be pulled out and used as a dining table or desk. An ottoman can serve as the footrest in a bedroom but be brought out to the living room as additional seating for guests. ■ Furniture will ideally be with you for a long time, so it's worth the effort to find the perfect piece.

Beds

BUNK BEDS are two single beds stacked one on top of the other. Most adults will not be happy in a bunk bed unless it is on a boat sailing to an exotic location. Bunk beds are space savers and are mostly used for a child's room, in a dormitory, or on a boat. It is a good idea for the top bunk to have a guard-rail to prevent the occupant from rolling out. The top bunk can be difficult to get into and out of as well as to make. Bunk beds are sometimes the only option for getting two twin beds into a small room with limited floor space.

A **CANOPY BED** is a four-poster bed with a canopy of fabric overhead. (Alternately, the canopy can be hung from the ceiling.) Historically in Europe canopy beds have been a status symbol and were made using the most expensive fabrics available—silk damasks and brocades with gold and silver threads. They were very elaborate with heavy curtains completely enclosing the bed to keep the warmth in. With the advent of modern heating, the canopy became more decorative and less functional, sometimes supported by just two posts at the head of the bed and extending only a few feet. In warmer climates a canopy might be made of mosquito netting.

Canopy beds come in all sizes, from twin to king, and usually have a pretty valance that can be trimmed with fringe. The underside of the canopy and the inside of the curtains are generally lined in a different fabric. The underside can be shirred, or gathered, to a center sunburst or it can be pulled taut. If the bed has curtains, tie-backs on the posts allow them to be pulled aside. A shirred or pleated curtain can hang down from the canopy behind the headboard.

A canopy bed is formal and feminine, whether in a little girl's room or a master bedroom. While not a necessity, when budget permits, a canopy bed can be a great addition to a bedroom.

Lit à la Polonaise is a whimsical style of canopy bed that has a fabric dome on curved stretchers and elaborate upholstery details. The posts are sometimes embellished with ostrich plumes. Centuries ago it was fashionable for hosts to receive visitors while still in bed. This made the bed a particularly important piece of furniture. A lit à la polonaise is fanciful and must be custom-made but, if your budget permits, is beautiful and amusing. Originally the upholstery was silk damasks and brocades, but a simple cotton print also looks great.

DAYBEDS are narrow beds that, placed lengthwise against a wall, also function as sofas. They have headboards and footboards of equal height that double as arms for the sofa, and bolsters and pillows to lean against. In the French Empire style of the nineteenth century, daybeds were particularly in vogue. A well-known modern version was designed by twentieth-century architect Ludwig Mies van der Rohe and has a simple flat, armless surface with one bolster. Daybeds with a mattress and box spring are generally more comfortable to sleep on than a sofa bed, but sofa beds are not restricted to twin size. Daybeds can be great in an alcove, especially with bookcases on either side. Daybeds are perfect in a home office, a sitting room that doubles as a guestroom, or in a studio apartment where space is limited. With a daybed, consider the lighting necessary for reading in bed and being able to turn off the light without getting out of bed—wall-mounted lamps can be a successful solution.

FOUR-POSTER BEDS have two tall posts at the headboard and two tall posts at the footboard. (There are also low four-poster beds that have posts not much higher than the headboards and footboards.) Four-poster beds are the skeletons of canopy beds. They can be any size, from twin to king, and the frame can be painted or stained

wood or even metal. A four-poster bed lends an interesting vertical element and design detail to a room. The posts are traditionally topped with a finial, which is an ornamental knob that can be a simple sphere or quite ornate.

Rails

Rails connect the headboard and footboard on four-poster, canopy, and some sleigh beds and daybeds. Rails are typically about 8 inches wide. The box spring often sets into the rails supported by L-shaped brackets, called angle irons, which are anchored on the rails, as illustrated. In some cases the box spring rests on top of the rails. In this case, the box spring is notched around the posts—called a rabbet edge. The box spring should be upholstered if it rests on top of the rails because it will be visible. A bedskirt is not necessary if the rails are finished, but if you want to have one, it can go either over or under the rails. If the rails are unfinished, then you should have a bedskirt that goes over the rails.

HEADBOARDS and **FOOTBOARDS**, originally built into bed frames to keep the drafts away, can be wood, rattan, wicker, metal, or upholstered. An upholstered headboard is soft to lean against. Headboards and footboards can be straight or shaped along the top. The headboard need not be part of the bed frame. A narrow wooden door or an iron gate, for example, can be hung on the wall as a headboard. Beds often have a metal frame supporting the box spring and mattress to which a headboard and footboard can be secured. A headboard should not just be propped up between a bed and the wall; it should either be bolted to the bed frame, or hung on the wall.

MURPHY BEDS have a spring hinge that allows the mattress and frame to be stored vertically in a cabinet. William Murphy, who was a stage coach driver and tinkerer, invented his famous bed in the early 1900s. Murphy beds are available in all sizes and typically hinge from the head of the bed. You need enough flat wall space to accommodate the height and width of the bed within the cabinet. For rooms with low ceilings, there is a style that hinges from the side. Murphy beds work in tight quarters where every inch of floor space counts. They don't provide the additional seating that a sofa bed or daybed does, but they can be a good solution when freeing up floor space is critical. The finish of the cabinet should integrate with the design of the room and might be painted the color of the wall.

A **SLEIGH BED** has a curved headboard and footboard that resembles a horse-drawn sleigh. The frame is traditionally made of wood. They come in any standard bed size—from twin to king—and can be set in the middle of a room or pushed up against a wall. A twin sleigh bed placed lengthwise against a wall can be a form of daybed. A sleigh bed can go in any style of house and lends an interesting design element to a bedroom. It often has rails like a four-poster bed. There are charming sleigh beds made for children, in pint-sized proportions, which are low to the ground and perfect for a first bed.

SOFA BEDS are great for multi-use rooms and for small spaces. A daybed, practically speaking, can only have a twin mattress, but a sofa bed can have a full- or queen-size mattress. A sofa bed also provides comfortable seating. Due to the necessary mechanism that allows the bed to fold up into the sofa frame they are not as comfortable as daybeds with a box spring. Sofa beds can either have loose cushions on the seat and the back, or else they can have a tight back, meaning there are no separate cushions. A tight back on a sofa bed makes a comfortable headboard and means fewer pillows to take off and store when the bed is pulled out. A sofa bed can be covered with any durable upholstery-weight fabric.

TRUNDLE BEDS have a mattress on a frame with wheels that slides under a regular bed. The idea of a trundle bed dates back hundreds of years to when servants and children in Europe slept on beds that were stored during the day under the master's bed. With a trundle bed, you need to have enough floor space for the second bed to be pulled out. Trundle beds are great in children's rooms, as they leave more floor space for everyday use and can be pulled out for a sleepover. A less expensive alternative to a trundle bed is an inflatable mattress for guests. However, inflating the mattress is a bit more of a production than just rolling out a bed.

Cabinets

ARMOIRE is the French word for a cabinet that serves as a wardrobe, cupboard, closet, or linen press—also called a clothes press. Armoires are tall, freestanding units with doors, and usually of substantial proportions. They are fitted with shelves and a drawer or two and can have a pole for hanging clothes. Armoires were originally created because a house didn't have built-in closets. In the seventeenth century they went from being simply utilitarian to highly prized decorative items. Armoires can be used in any room and can be any style. They are useful as a media cabinet to house televisions, DVD players, and stereos. Unless you have a new armoire outfitted for this purpose, you will need to drill holes for wires and re-fit the shelves in an old armoire. It is well worth the effort. If you have a valuable antique armoire, consult with a trusted antique dealer or appraiser before drilling holes and moving shelves. An armoire is well suited to a bedroom that otherwise lacks proper storage space. Another good use for an armoire is as a bar in a living room or library.

BREAKFRONTS are tall cabinets so named because the center section breaks forward, usually 3 to 4 inches, making it deeper than the side sections. The breakfront was originally produced in eighteenth-century England and used in dining rooms to store flatware, linen, and place settings. These tall cabinets are generally in two separate pieces, an upper and a lower section. Larger breakfronts might even have more sections. The lower half usually has a pair of solid doors with shelves or drawers behind, and the upper section has shelves with glass-paned doors that are a wonderful way to display porcelain or other decorative objects. Often the interior of the upper section is lined in fabric or painted a color that complements the room. A breakfront also can be lighted for purposes of display.

CORNER CABINETS have a triangular shape that fits snugly into a corner. It is a traditional form that is usually tall and used for storage or display. Corner cabinets are seen in English, French, and American styles and can be painted or stained wood. They have shelves and often doors and frequently lend a rustic feel. A corner cabinet can make a room feel cozier by filling up an empty corner. A corner cabinet is perfect for storing and displaying dishes in a country-style dining room.

CREDENZA is an Italian antique form used as a sideboard in a dining room. Today, a long and low piece of furniture placed next to a desk is also called a credenza. The original credenza derived from the credence, a small side table used in churches to hold items for Mass. Today you are most likely to see a credenza in an office behind a desk.

A **LINEN PRESS**, also called a Clothes Press, is a type of wardrobe, or armoire, that was originally placed in the laundry room of a house so that after a beautiful tablecloth, for example, had been washed and ironed, it could be hung until it was used. Linen presses are old-fashioned linen closets, not a fancy form but instead likely to have been made by a country cabinetmaker. They are often made of a modest wood, such as pine, without much detail. The upper section of a linen press has hanging space and on the bottom are shelves or drawers for storing folded linens. As discussed with armoires, a refurbished linen press is very useful as a cabinet to house a TV or stereo equipment and CDs. They are perfect in a bedroom with inadequate closet space.

Chairs

ARMCHAIR is a generic term for any chair with arms, whether it be all-upholstered or with a wooden frame. Generally people are happy to sit in an armchair for longer than in a side chair, which has no arms, as it is more comfortable.

The **BARCELONA CHAIR** was designed by the German-born architect Ludwig Mies van der Rohe (1886–1969) and made its debut in 1929 at the German pavilion of the Barcelona International Exhibition. A daybed and a footstool were also designed in the same style as the Barcelona chair. They have a chrome-plated steel frame and buttoned leather cushions. Barcelona chairs are comfortable and modern. In a living room or sitting room, they are great, either next to a sofa or instead of a sofa. They have a pared-down look and are best suited to similarly uncluttered settings.

The **BENTWOOD CHAIR** was developed by Michael Thonet in Germany in the 1830s using a process of steaming wood to soften and bend it. This was one of the first mass-produced pieces of furniture. Thonet Industries went on to produce classic designs for modern architects and furniture designers such as Ludwig Mies van der Rohe and Marcel Breuer (1902–1981). To this day Thonet makes mass-produced furniture. The bentwood technique has been used for a wide variety of designs—from armchairs to rocking chairs—but Thonet's original cafe chair is still widely seen. The proportions of a bentwood cafe chair are such that you can use them nicely in small spaces. They lend themselves to a kitchen or a simple country dining room. Delicate and distinctive, they are still often seen in restaurants and cafes.

BERGÈRE is a style of French upholstered armchair with a wooden frame. The distinguishing feature of a bergère is the closed, upholstered sides below the arms. The frame and legs are often carved and have a painted, stained, or gilded finish. They are classic, elegant chairs still widely reproduced. Bergères are most suitable in a living room, sitting room, or bedroom, and should have a tight upholstered back and either a tight seat or a loose seat cushion. The upholstery fabric can be almost anything as long as the scale of the print isn't too big for the chair. Leather, velvet, tapestry, toile, and chintz are all suitable fabrics.

A **CHAISE LONGUE**, which means "long chair" in French, can be made in one piece or two as a chair and ottoman. The original chaise longue was one piece with a carved wooden frame that was often upholstered with silk brocade or damask. The form gained much popularity in the eighteenth century as a boudoir piece. Today it is still perfect in the corner of a bedroom—a great place to put your feet up and read. The chaise longue has evolved through the centuries and modern styles have been designed. Thonet Industries, a leading modern furniture producer, made steel and bentwood chaise longues, for example. In its traditional form, a chaise longue is a feminine piece of furniture; you don't picture a burly man plopping onto a chaise longue for a quick nap. Over time the chaise longue has found its way from the boudoir into living rooms and libraries and can be more efficient when in two pieces, as you can move the ottoman around as needed. Any upholstery-weight fabric is suitable: velvet, chintz, silk, or plain cotton fabric are a few. Also, the chaise longue is a staple by a pool but is made from more weatherproof materials.

DINING CHAIRS are any chair at a dining table. They can be armchairs or side chairs, though it's a generally good idea, as it looks more finished, to have armchairs at the ends of a rectangular dining table. When considering dining chairs, no matter how formal your dining room or dining area, keep in mind comfort and durability. A dinner party held on uncomfortable chairs is sure to end quickly. Also, the chairs should bear the largest guest you might have, even if he rocks back to make the great point of the evening. Check that the chairs are compatible with the height of the dining table—no one likes to feel as if his or her chin is nearly resting in the soup. Also, if the dining table has an apron, which is a horizontal support for the tabletop (see page 106), make sure there is plenty of space for people's legs between the chair seat and the bottom of the apron—approximately 9 inches is good.

FAUTEUIL is a French-style armchair with a wooden frame and open arms, meaning there is open space between the arm and the seat. It will have a tight back, meaning there is no separate back cushion, and can have either a tight seat or a loose seat cushion. Fauteuils might have the

outside of the back upholstered in a less expensive fabric, which was customary in the eighteenth century. You might have a pair of fauteuils with a table between them, or you could have one or a pair on either side of a sofa. A single fauteuil can help round out a furniture grouping in the living room or be tucked into the corner of a bedroom. Many upholstery fabrics, from leather to brocade, are suitable for a fauteuil. Some fauteuils have caning on the seat and back, which is very pretty.

A **KLISMOS CHAIR** is an ancient Greek design where the back of the chair is concave to fit the contour of the body. The Neoclassical resurgence in the eighteenth and nineteenth centuries made the klismos popular again, and in the 1940s a furniture designer named T. H. Robsjohn-Gibbings, among others, used the klismos shape frequently in his designs. It is an example of how a clean, simple design will always endure. The style is well suited to a contemporary look and can be used as a dining chair; a particularly good combination is klismos dining chairs around a stone-topped table. Also, a pair of klismos chairs can be used in a hallway or a living room on either side of a table. Klismos chairs come with and without arms. It's the shape of the back and the legs that define it.

LADDER-BACK CHAIRS have horizontal wooden supports resembling a ladder on the back of the chair. This style was used often in mid-eighteenth-century England; the chairs were made from mahogany and had a tight upholstered seat (see illustration). An American version of the style developed with more of a country look. This style has a high back and often a rush seat. A leather seat with nail head trimming looks great on the more formal English style. No cushion is necessary with a rush seat on the American version, but a flat loose cushion in a simple cotton fabric is suitable. Both styles make great dining chairs.

PEACOCK CHAIRS are so called because the back resembles a peacock with its tail in full bloom. They are typically made of wicker or rattan. It is an amusing shape with a light and airy feel. There are different styles of the peacock chair. Some have relatively low backs while other chairs might have backs up to five feet high. They are great in hot climates or beach houses when you have a ceiling fan overhead and a cool drink nearby. Peacock chairs could be used as end chairs at a dining table or on a covered porch or a living room. They can be painted any color, and a seat cushion can be made from any informal fabric — batiks or heavy cotton with an exotic print work well.

ROCKING CHAIRS have an all-American look that seems to jump straight out of a Norman Rockwell illustration. Early forms of the rocking chair were the Windsor rocking chairs and the Boston Rocker. The earliest rockers were in nurseries. The rocking chair is a comfort chair, and, besides in a baby's room, can be great on a porch or in a library. One thing to remember is there needs to be enough space around the chair so the rails don't hit walls or furniture if someone is rocking.

SIDE CHAIR is a generic term for a chair without arms. Side chairs can be any style — from a classic English ladder back to a Hepplewhite-style chair to a klismos chair — even a metal folding chair could be considered a side chair. In the twentieth century, side chairs were designed by architects and furniture designers such as Charles and Ray Eames, Charles Rennie Mackintosh, and Frank Lloyd Wright, to name just a few. They can be used as dining chairs, as hall chairs, as desk chairs, or as additional seating.

SLIPPER CHAIRS are upholstered chairs with slender proportions and no arms. The beauty of slipper chairs is that they are comfortable and take up less space than a regular upholstered chair. They are perfect in a bedroom, living room, or library, and have an elegant coziness that is perfect in smaller rooms. Any upholstery fabric is suitable from chintz, to toile de jouy, to velvet, to a simple woven fabric. However, since the chair typically has petite proportions, the scale of the pattern on the fabric should also be relatively small or even a solid color.

TÊTE À TÊTES seat two people facing each other. In French the name means "head to head." Upholstered tête à têtes were seen in salons in the eighteenth and nineteenth centuries, and today they are a wonderful addition in a living room. Tête à têtes are a seldom-used but amusing piece of furniture. They are designed to be placed in the center of a room. The upholstery fabric can be silk velvet, damask, brocade, or a plain silk. Cotton fabric can also be used. A tête à tête may have a wonderful fringe around the bottom. A variation of the tête à tête chair is the dos à dos chair (in French literally "back to back"). This chair seats two people facing away from one another and is another type of chair that can be a conversation piece in and of itself.

The **TULIP CHAIR** was designed by the influential Finnish-born American architect Eero Saarinen (1910–1961) in 1956 and is still widely seen today. He also used the pedestal of the tulip chair on tables and other styles of chairs. Tulip chairs have a simple design that can be dressed up or down in a modern setting. They come with or without a swivel and make good dining chairs or side chairs in a living room. The cushion gives a splash of color.

UPHOLSTERED ARMCHAIRS are unbeatable for pure comfort. They come in a variety of styles; often used are Bridgewater, Lawson, Marshall Field, and Odom, to name a few. They can have tight seats and backs or loose seat and back cushions, which can be filled with down and feathers, or a polyester blend, or a combination.

These chairs can be on swivels, which is very nice in a living room or library for turning to watch television. An upholstered armchair is great in the corner of a bedroom, with or without a matching ottoman, for reading by a window. Different styles of upholstered chairs and sofas are discussed further in the chapter on upholstery.

WINDSOR CHAIRS are wooden chairs with distinctive spindle backs. Originally an English style, they were adapted and widely produced in America starting in the mid-eighteenth century, and were so popular that even George Washington had them at Mount Vernon. They come in a few different styles and sizes and can be made by hand or machine. They come either with or without arms. Windsor chairs lend themselves to a traditional country style and are quite comfortable even without a loose seat cushion. Antique Windsor chairs and reproductions are both available. They are perfect in a dining room, living room, library, or at a desk.

WING CHAIRS are upholstered armchairs on legs, with tall backs and the distinguishing feature of wings along the sides of the back. The wings were originally designed as protection against drafts and were noted as being comfortable for naps. These chairs were first called "easy chairs" in late seventeenth-century England. Wing chairs are well suited for a library or a living room. They are a particularly good for sitting by a fire or in a corner for reading by a window. Since the back of the chair is quite high, it is best

placed near a wall and not in the center of the room. Wing chairs can be covered in any fabric suitable for upholstery, with either a nail head or gimp trimming.

Chair Details

RUSH SEATS were originally made from cattail or bulrush woven to create a resilient seat. Cattails and bulrushes are still used to make rush seats, but they are relatively expensive and only seasonally available. Since the early 1900s rush

A Few Influential English Cabinetmakers

While there have been many highly talented cabinetmakers and furniture designers through the ages, three eighteenth-century English cabinetmakers stand out as particularly influential. These cabinetmakers developed distinctive styles that are widely seen in reproductions today.

Thomas Chippendale (1718–1779) published *The Gentleman and Cabinet-Maker's Director* in 1754. Chippendale worked mostly in mahogany and with so-called japanned, meaning a faux lacquer finish, furniture in a chinoiserie style. He was one of the first great, widely known cabinetmakers.

George Hepplewhite (d. 1786) wrote *The Cabinet-maker and Upholsterer's Guide,* which was published posthumously in 1788. Hepplewhite was known for using satinwood and for his graceful curved designs. Hepplewhite was influenced at least in part by the great *ébénistes,* or cabinetmakers, of France.

Thomas Sheraton (1751–1806) published *The Cabinet-Maker and Upholsterer's Drawing-Book* in 1791. Known for rectilinear lines and delicate proportions, he was influenced greatly by Chippendale, Hepplewhite, and the designs of the Louis XVI period.

seats have been made using paper fiber, and this type of seat is most common today. Rush seats are seen on many types of chairs; American ladder-back chairs and rocking chairs will often have them. The rush can either be wrapped around the frame of the chair or around a slip seat, which has a separate frame that is dropped into the seat of the chair. There are a variety of natural colors to choose from. A seat can be re-rushed, which is a good pick-me-up for a flea market find.

SLIP SEAT is a chair seat that can be dropped into and lifted out of the frame of the chair. It can be either upholstered or rushed. It used to be that different seats were used for different seasons or just for a change of pace. Slip seats make recovering a seat much easier as the chair can stay put and the seat alone can be sent out. Slip seats are practical, but only certain chairs are designed to have them.

Chests

BLANKET CHESTS have a simple design and traditionally were placed at the end of a bed. Centuries ago, chests were needed for storage and for travel, as a precursor to the modern-day suitcase. Chests were also used for seating. The blanket chest in particular is an American form, seen in Shaker and early American styles. A flat cushion can be put on top of a chest so it can double as a seat. For toy storage in a child's room, towel storage in a bathroom, blankets at the end of a bed, or as a coffee table in a living room, a blanket chest is a useful and versatile piece of furniture.

CHEST ON CHEST is a tall chest in two parts. The lower section is slightly larger than the upper section. It is an antique form and is similar to a high boy but doesn't have legs. A chest on chest is useful in a bedroom but can also be attractive in a hall or a living room. Originally an English form, it was also popular in America.

A **COMMODE** is a French chest that stands on legs and generally has two or three drawers and a marble top. It was first widely seen in France in the early eighteenth century. In French, *commode* means "convenient." A commode often has a serpentine, or curved, front and beautiful mounts and hardware, which can make it quite ornate. A commode is frequently seen in a formal front hall or a living room, sometimes flanked by a pair of side chairs. It is an elegant piece of furniture — the greatest cabinetmakers in France made commodes.

HIGHBOY is a tall chest of drawers on legs. It has separate upper and lower sections that rest on top of each other but are not joined. The highboy — also called a Tall Boy — was first seen in England during the late seventeenth century and, later, widely seen in America. As with much furniture from that time, it was made in two pieces to facilitate moving it. The name highboy is thought to come from the English mispronunciation of *bois*, the French word for "wood." Highboys are seen in many styles. It is a versatile form. In a dining room it provides useful storage space for table linens and settings. At the end of a long hall, it can be a good focal point; or in an entrance hall it's visually interesting. The lower section of a highboy, if it has a finished top, is called a lowboy.

Desks

A **KNEEHOLE DESK** has an open space for the knees between two pedestals. A pedestal desk is another name for this style. The top of a knee-hole desk is often covered with leather and the pedestals will have drawers, shelves, or shelves behind doors. The back of the kneehole space can either be finished or left open. A kneehole desk is perfect in a library, a bedroom, or a home office. The form dates back to the eighteenth century, but contemporary versions of the design are frequently seen. It is a timeless design because it is useful and comfortable, with plenty of legroom and storage space. If the back of the desk is finished, it can be placed perpendicular to the wall; if not, then the back must be placed against the wall. A modern, simple version of the kneehole desk can be created by topping two filing cabinets with a wooden board that can be stained, painted, or covered in a plastic laminate.

A **PARTNERS DESK** is a larger version of a kneehole desk that is designed for two people to sit facing each other. There are drawers or shelves on both sides of the pedestals. A partners desk must be placed perpendicularly to the wall or in the center of a room. This design is most useful in an office or library setting. While there are beautiful antique partners desks available, the design can be recreated using filing cabinets and a wooden top that can be painted, stained, or covered with a plastic laminate.

A **ROLLTOP DESK** is defined by a wooden cover that rolls down over the writing surface on a curved track. It has pigeonholes, which are small compartments built into the desktop for storing letters and such. A rolltop desk is an eighteenth-century design that traditionally is delicate, more for a lady's bedroom than for a leather and tweed library. A traditional rolltop desk is a perfect place to write thank you notes. That said, it's possible to find one with rather large proportions — but it isn't typical of the original style.

A **SECRETARY** is a tall cabinet made in two parts, with a writing surface hidden behind a false drawer that can be pulled out of the lower section. The drawer front hinges down, and the slide pulls out. The upper section has shelves behind glass-paned or solid-wood doors. The shelves provide a great place to display books or decorative objects. Beneath the writing surface are two or three long drawers. Secretaries were particularly popular in eighteenth-century England and were generally made in mahogany. The form has a traditional, somewhat formal look. A secretary is practical since you can do deskwork at it and then conceal the writing surface. Since it is tall, a secretary lends a good vertical element to the design of a room. In a more contemporary setting, instead of a secretary, you might see a built-in desk with shelves above.

A **SLANT-TOP DESK** is a chest of drawers with a writing surface that hinges down from a slanted position and onto two supports that pull out from the frame. This type of desk typically has pigeonholes, which are small compartments built into the desktop for holding letters and such. In a hallway, a library, a bedroom, or a living room, this type of desk can be useful and attractive.

A **WRITING TABLE** stands on legs and has drawers built into the apron, which is the horizontal support below the top. It is a French form from the eighteenth century, traditionally called a bureau plat, although English variations were also made. *Bureau plat* means "flat desk" in French. A writing table has a lighter look than other desks. A Parsons table, which is a streamlined twentieth-century design where the legs and the apron are flush and of equal size, can be made in proportions similar to an antique writing table. A Parsons table can be made with either no drawers or a concealed drawer in the apron. Such a table can double as a dining table in a small space.

Furniture Details

The **APRON** is the horizontal support directly below a tabletop. Too wide an apron will make it difficult to get your legs comfortably under the table when you sit at it. Adequate legroom requires that between the bottom of the table apron and the top of a chair seat there should be approximately 9 inches.

Creating Conversation Groupings

Living rooms and sitting rooms, no matter the style, should be conducive to socializing, whether it's just family or a full-blown party. The furniture layout and lighting are important in achieving this goal.

A conversation grouping generally has a sofa with a coffee table in front of it and chairs on either end of the coffee table. In a large room you might have two or three conversation groupings. It is a good idea to have some side chairs or ottomans that can easily be pulled up to join a grouping. Having an ottoman on casters, which are small wheels, can make this easier. Tables should be placed so that you can conveniently put a drink down or pick up a book. Sofas and chairs should be close enough to each other to allow a comfortable conversation.

Living rooms and sitting rooms should have one or two good reading lamps as well as background lighting fixtures that can be dimmed to create ambiance. Wall sconces and ceiling fixtures are ideal for background lighting. In a more contemporary setting, recessed and track lights are suitable.

The **BOMBÉ** shape is a curved swelling through the middle of a piece of furniture—often a commode or a chest of drawers. French and Italian furniture in the eighteenth century often had a bombé shape, particularly during the Rococo period. The bombé shape has been used widely— from Dutch to English design—and is still seen today. The shape adds interest and a European flair to a piece of furniture.

CABRIOLE LEGS are curved to resemble an animal leg with a knee, ankle, and foot. They were widely used in English and European furniture design in the late seventeenth and early eighteenth centuries. In French, *cabriole* means "leap" or "caper," and the cabriole leg was thought to resemble a leaping or playful animal. At the knee there is often an embellishment, a carved shell motif, for example. Cabriole legs were used on different types of furniture—from chairs to chests. By the late eighteenth and early nineteenth centuries, cabriole legs went out of fashion and were replaced by straight legs typical of the Neoclassical resurgence. Much reproduction furniture today uses the cabriole leg.

CANING is a material of open weave made with strong reeds. It adds an interesting texture to furniture and is seen on the seats and backs of chairs, on screens, tabletops, and headboards, for example. Caning can be done by hand or by machine. Traditional caning is done by hand, and the reed is woven through holes in the frame of the piece of furniture. The newer method of caning uses a pre-woven sheet that is secured into a groove in the frame of the furniture. The pre-woven caning is held in place by a spline, which is a flexible wedge-shaped strip. The traditional caning pattern is a hexagram, but more elaborate and intricate weaving patterns also exist. Caning gives a lighter feeling to a piece of furniture than, for example, solid wood. If you have a piece of furniture where the caning is coming apart, there are places that will re-cane surfaces, either by hand or by using the pre-woven sheets. If you spot a great chair frame with caning in disrepair, it might be well worth fixing it up.

CASTERS are small wheels attached to the bottom or the legs of a piece of furniture such as an upholstered chair, a sofa, a table, or an ottoman. It's a good idea to have casters on any piece of furniture that you might want to move around but is too heavy to be easily lifted. For example, if you're entertaining, it's great to have one or two small pieces of furniture that can be easily pulled up to expand a group. An ottoman on casters is perfect for this. A side chair is also good to pull up to round out a group but would not be put on casters because it can easily be lifted and moved. Larger casters that lock are used on bed frames.

FRETWORK is an ornamental design with angular elements. Fretwork is traditionally in a band; a Greek key motif is often used, for example. It is also seen on the rectangular door of a cabinet. When the segments of the design are set on the diagonal, the fretwork tends to take on an Asian look. The eighteenth-century English cabinet-maker Thomas Chippendale often used fretwork in his chair and cabinet designs.

FURNITURE FEET come in a wide array of forms. Late seventeenth- and early eighteenth-century furniture tended to have more elaborately carved feet than furniture made later in the eighteenth century during the Neoclassical and Empire periods.

The **Ball and Claw Foot** is thought to be adapted from a Chinese design and represents a clawed dragon holding a pearl of wisdom. This form is used with a cabriole leg and is seen in English and some Dutch furniture from the late seventeenth and early to mid-eighteenth centuries. It was especially typical of the Queen Anne style in England during that time.

The **Bracket Foot** is an angular, square-shaped support for cabinets and tables that was originally used in the eighteenth century. The English cabinetmaker Thomas Chippendale used a bracket foot in his designs. The bracket foot is seen in English, European, and American furniture design.

The **Bun Foot** looks like a partly flattened sphere and is seen frequently on chests, tables, and sofas. It was first seen on English and European furniture in the late seventeenth century.

The **Club Foot**, or Pad Foot, is a simple rounded foot that was widely seen with a cabriole leg in England in the late seventeenth and early eighteenth centuries during the Queen Anne and Early Georgian periods.

The **Spade Foot** is a simple square that tapers toward the floor. It was often seen in the late eighteenth-century designs of English cabinet-makers George Hepplewhite and Thomas Sheraton, to name just two. The spade foot gained popularity during the Neoclassical period.

PEDIMENT is an ornamental element seen at the top of traditional antique forms such as a breakfront, highboy, or secretary. It is also a Classical architectural element that projects out over windows and doors on the exteriors of buildings. It can be triangular, curved, or broken, meaning that the topmost section is cut out and sometimes is filled with an ornament such as an urn.

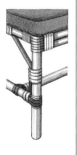

RATTAN is a particular plant—from the palm family, genus Calamus—that is used to make furniture. It is similar to wicker, but has a light, airy, more Asian look. Rattan can be stained or left its natural color. Rattan is not often finished with paint, as wicker is, in part because it has a tougher, less porous skin than wicker and so does not absorb paint as well. Paint will help to protect wicker whereas paint is more likely to chip off of rattan.

A **SERPENTINE CURVE** may be seen on the front of a piece of furniture such as a chest of drawers, a commode, or a console table.

Serpentine describes anything with S-shaped curves. A serpentine curve is seen on English, European, and American furniture. A camelback sofa, for example, has a serpentine curve (it is illustrated on page 176).

SPLAT is a vertical piece of wood in the center of the back of a chair which can be shaped or carved. Some styles of side chairs have elaborately carved splats, while other styles may have a simple strip of wood. In Asian-style chairs you will see a straight splat that is not carved.

STRETCHERS connect and brace the legs on a piece of furniture, usually a few inches off the floor. Stretchers have different designs. An H stretcher—two braces that connect the front legs to the back legs on each side and a third brace that runs across the middle—is typical.

WICKER is woven plant material used to make furniture—from tables to chairs to headboards. It is relatively inexpensive and can be painted. White painted wicker is ideal in a summerhouse. Other colors that look great on wicker are black, dark green, or slate gray. Wicker furniture is frequently seen on a covered porch in the summer.

Furniture Finishes

GILDING is the process of adding gold to the surface of wood or metal. It has a sophisticated look and is used on some of the finest antiques, decorative objects, hardware, and metalwork. Gilded bronze is called ormolu and was used often by the French. Gilding is still done today. There are two methods: **water gilding** and **oil gilding**. Water gilding is the older, more time-consuming technique that can be burnished—made very bright. Oil gilding has a more matte finish than water gilding. In eighteenth-century Europe, water gilding was often burnished to a

Finials

Finials are the ornamental knobs at the end of a pole or post. You see finials in many places: on the posts of a four-poster bed, on top of some lamps to secure the lampshade, on the ends of curtain poles, and on newel posts. They come in a wide variety of styles and materials and can range from simple to elaborately carved and gilded.

Finials add a finishing touch and can be an interesting detail in a room. A carved green jade finial on top of a lamp can lend an Asian look, for example. Common motifs for finials are pinecones and urns, to name just a couple. In a pared-down setting finials should be simple—a basic sphere perhaps. There are entire catalogues dedicated to finials. The important thing is that the finial suits the piece it is on and complements the overall look of the room.

high dazzling shine. Today you are more likely to see gilding that is not so shiny—it's a matter of taste. When restoring fine antiques, there may be a technique, either water gilding or oil gilding, which will be more appropriate to use for a specific piece. For example, if you have a gilded mirror frame from eighteenth-century France, water gilding burnished to brilliance will probably most closely resemble the original finish. For other antique pieces, oil gilding may be better suited. An antique dealer or restorer would know which method is best to use. With both methods, the gold can vary from a silvery to a reddish color.

In water gilding, a layer of clay, called the bole coat, is applied over a layer of gesso, which is a white paste also used as a base coat for oil paint on a canvas. The bole coat can be red, yellow, gray, or sometimes black. Since gold leaf is somewhat transparent, the color of the bole coat will come through. With some antiques, it may be possible to tell their country of origin from the color of the clay used for the bole coat.

In oil gilding, a layer of color can be put down under the gold leaf. Red-toned gold is particularly beautiful.

Silver leaf can also be used for highlights through a process called **silvering**. This can be quite beautiful, but the silver must be sealed or it will tarnish. An alternative is using silver-colored gold, which will not tarnish.

If you find a piece of furniture at auction or at a flea market, gilding can breathe new life into it. For less lavish budgets, something close to the effect of gilding can be achieved using paints and glazes.

INLAY is a decorative finish where fine materials are inserted into the surface of an object, giving it more color and added interest. Inlay work has been used for thousands of years. Metal, stone, or wood—such as satinwood, rosewood, and ebony—can be inlaid into a surface. Spanish-style furniture often has silver and ivory inlay, while much Italian Renaissance furniture has intricate wood inlay. The seams between the inlaid pieces should be virtually invisible and the surface flush. If a piece of inlay is starting to pop up, put it in an envelope or drawer until it can easily be glued back into place, because it will be difficult to replace if it's lost.

LACQUER is a type of finish originally made from the sap of the Rhus tree, indigenous to China. It creates a hard, glossy, and smooth surface. For a long time lacquer was known to Europe only through imports; European climates couldn't support the Rhus tree and the sap was impossible to ship from the Far East. An imitation of the lacquered finish was developed in the seventeenth century, and in about 1660 "japanned" furniture, made with a fake lacquer finish, was first seen in England. In 1688 John Stalker and George Parker published a book titled *A Treatise of Japanning and Varnishing* that included recipes for lacquer substitutes and designs for making japanned furniture.

Lacquer, or imitation lacquer, was widely seen in the French Rococo and English Regency periods. The eighteenth-century English cabinetmaker Thomas Chippendale designed many japanned pieces. What we call lacquer today is still often imitation lacquer—the effect can be achieved with newer high-gloss paints or multiple layers of varnish. The high-gloss look of lacquer has a formal feel and a lacquered piece, whether it's a mirror frame or a table, can add visual interest to a room. Be forewarned that the shine of lacquer exponentially magnifies any imperfections on the surface, so it should only be used on perfectly smooth surfaces.

PAINTED FINISHES can be anything from a solid color to an elaborate design, a lacquered high-gloss finish to a milk paint matte finish. A fresh coat of paint can bring new life to an old piece of furniture. The final result depends greatly on the preparation. It's important to carefully sand and to thoroughly clean the surface before painting. Gilding, or a similar highlight or accent, can be added to finer pieces—a little metal can add elegance. Decorative finishes such as faux wood or stone can be used quite beautifully. With faux finishes it's a good rule of thumb to use the faux only where the real material might be used—a tabletop might really be stone (and therefore suitable for a faux stone paint treatment), but the frame of a chair would not be made of stone.

PATINA is the film, or glow, of age, which develops over time on objects, from wood furniture and paneling to the facade of a house to a bronze sculpture. It develops from exposure to air and the elements, from being handled, and from the residue of cleaning and waxing. A patina mellows colors and can add value to an antique. It would be a mistake to strip the patina off an antique — some of the value might be stripped away as well. It's possible to fake a patina, using glaze among other things, which tones down the color and creates a more irregular surface texture.

VENEER is a thin layer of a decorative material, wood or synthetic, that is laid over a sub-surface, thus giving a finer finish. Veneers are found on furniture, floors, and walls. Some of the finest eighteenth-century English furniture is veneered. A veneer allows for a particularly beautiful piece of wood to be used on more than one piece of furniture. It also means that multiple pieces of furniture can have a nearly identical surface. Some pieces of furniture, antique or not, have "book matched" veneers, where two pieces of veneer from the same piece of wood are placed next to each other as essentially a mirror image. Today, plastic laminates are used as veneers on kitchen counters, for example. Many types of wood flooring are made using veneers. The veneer on furniture can be replaced, either the whole piece or just a section. You are more likely to replace the veneer on furniture than you are to sand and refinish it, because a veneer is often too thin to sand. On floors, you might be able to sand the veneer for refinishing up to a few times, but otherwise the veneer will have to be replaced if it is damaged.

Ottomans and Benches

A **BANQUETTE** is an upholstered bench that is made to fit into a particular space. Restaurants frequently have a long banquette that runs the length of an entire wall. A banquette can also fit into an alcove or bay window. It can be curved, have two or more sections, and be either all upholstered or have a wood frame and loose cushions. It can have an upholstered back or no back. A banquette is a superb and comfortable solution for an alcove. It also makes a great window seat. The fabric covering a banquette can dress it up or down. Upholstery material should be suitably durable: corduroy, tapestry, chenille, or any strong woven fabric will work. The seat of the banquette can be designed to lift up to create additional storage space.

A **DEACON'S BENCH** is quite narrow and not particularly comfortable. It is traditionally used in a church, Quaker meeting hall, or similar venue. But a deacon's bench can also be great in a front hall or mudroom as a place to throw a coat, or to sit and put on shoes. A hook board could be hung on the wall above for coats and hats, and boots, clogs, and shoes can be stored below. It looks cozy, and for comfort, you can put a thin flat cushion on the seat. You might find a deacon's bench at a flea market, auction, or country antique shop.

A **FENDER BENCH** is designed to go around the hearth of a fireplace. The base is made of metal—brass, steel, or iron. The seat is narrow and upholstered with leather, suede, horsehair cloth, or fabric. The seat can either run straight, parallel to the fireplace, or it can be U-shaped and return to the wall. The bench can be all one height or it can dip in the center to make tending the fire easier. It is attractive to trim a bench like this with nail heads. A fender bench is a place to sit while tending the fire or warming up. One thinks of a fender bench as part of the sporting life—a place to sit after coming in from a pheasant shoot or tramping in the moors. A fender bench, which gives additional seating in a room without taking up much space, can be nicely used around any fireplace. It works best if custom fitted to the hearth but also comes in standard sizes.

An **OTTOMAN** is a low upholstered seat that doesn't have a back. It is a versatile piece of furniture, either standing on its own or going with a matching upholstered chair to create a chaise longue. In a living room an ottoman can be used as an additional surface for newspapers and magazines or serve as a foot rest after a long day. Having an ottoman by a bedroom chair is perfect for a quick nap or for reading by a window. While an ottoman alone is not great for sinking into, it is a good way to add additional seating to a room without taking up much space. If you're entertaining, an ottoman can easily be pulled up to join a group, and can be put on casters for this purpose. An ottoman also works well in front of a fireplace, as it doesn't block the heat or the view of the fire. There are many ottoman styles: it can be on legs with an upholstered seat or all-upholstered with an upholstered platform instead of legs. The seat on an all-upholstered ottoman can be a tight seat with or without tufting or it can have a separate loose seat cushion, which makes it more comfortable and casual.

Screens

A screen has two or more hinged panels and stands on its own. It is a great way to divide space or to hide things such as a television or a door to a kitchen. Versatile and useful, a screen can be used as a decorative element to fill an empty corner or in a bedroom to conceal a dressing area or bed. There are a nearly endless number of options

for a screen: it can be covered in mirror for an Art Deco or urban look; covered with leather and trimmed with nail heads for a library; or embellished with hooks for hats in a hallway. It can be short or tall. It can be upholstered with any upholstery fabric. You could use a corkboard-covered screen to conceal a desk, or a wooden screen could be painted with a trompe-l'oeil scene for a dining room. A screen with four or more panels can be divided into two smaller screens and used to decorate two corners in a room. A Japanese shoji-style screen with paper panels on a wooden frame has a simple look. A screen with a wooden frame and glass panes has a particularly French look and is meant to block drafts but not light. Scenic wallpaper or tea paper can be put on a screen.

Settees and Sofas

Settees and sofas are staples in the house. Settees are the precursor to the modern all-upholstered sofa. There are many styles of upholstered sofas; some are detailed in the upholstery chapter.

A **KNOLE SOFA** has a high back and arms of equal height. The first knole sofa was made in the early to mid seventeenth century for Knole, a house in Kent, England. Knole is now a National Trust Property and the original sofa is still there—covered in red velvet and trimmed with nail heads. It was originally used in a very formal setting. The upholstered arms hinge from the base and can be lowered or held upright with a cord tied around finials on the back. This detail, it is believed, was designed to accommodate the large dresses that women wore at the time. A knole sofa is stylish and mixes well with many different looks. Typically it has bun feet, trimmed with tape, cord, or nail heads, and with a round bolster inside each of the arms. The finials can be either carved wood or covered in fabric. Any fabric suitable for upholstery, from a brocade to cotton print, depending on the setting, works well. See Chapter 9: Upholstery for more sofa styles.

A **SETTEE** is an early form of the modern sofa and has a wooden frame. It typically has an upholstered seat, 4 to 6 legs, open arms, and a carved or upholstered back. The length varies. The seat height of a traditional settee is the same as a side chair, which is generally higher than a sofa. A settee is great in a hallway to throw a coat on. There are settees made in a contemporary style, but the form is very traditional. The all-upholstered sofa has taken over for everyday use and is generally more comfortable and less formal. The upholstery fabric can be anything from silk damask to velvet to leather to a cotton print. The scale of the fabric's print—if it has one—should match the proportions of the settee. A nail head trim or gimp (a braided trimming) are both suitable.

Stools

BAR STOOLS are tall seats on legs with or without a back. They are seen most often in a row at a bar, but tall stools are also very useful in a

Buying a Comfortable Sofa

Selecting a good, comfortable sofa is an important priority. There are some general guidelines for finding the most comfortable sofa in your price range. The depth of the seat cushions should be approximately 24 to 26 inches. The height of the back should be about 28 to 31 inches off the floor. An average seat height is 18 to 20 inches off the floor, which should be comfortable for most people.

The real test, though, is to sit in the sofa and to see for yourself how comfortable it is.

house. A stool can be tucked under a counter to conserve space and pulled out when needed. People generally like to sit up high, and the compact design is useful in a small space.

FOOTSTOOLS were originally used to help keep people's feet off cold and drafty floors. Today a footstool can be a comfortable way to put your feet up. They are small and can be tucked away more easily than an ottoman. Footstools come in a wide variety of styles from the traditional form of a wooden frame with a tight or tufted upholstered top to a contemporary style that might have a metal frame and no cushion. A footstool with leather and a nail head trim has a traditional look well suited to a library. A tuffet is another name for a footstool—as in Little Miss Muffet sat on her tuffet . . .

Tables

A **BUTLER'S TRAY TABLE** has a tray that fits into a stand. It was originally designed for serving food and drinks. The stand can either be low for use as a coffee table or higher for use as a bar. This traditional English design is widely seen today, especially as a coffee table. The tabletop generally has hinged flaps along the sides that flip up to facilitate carrying. A butler's tray table suits a traditional room.

COFFEE TABLE is a generic term for a low table that goes in front of a sofa. It is placed at the center of a conversation grouping. The coffee table is a relatively new form of furniture, designed to be compatible with an upholstered sofa, which was first seen in the mid- to late nineteenth century. The table height ideally should be the same or slightly lower than the seat of the sofa. Antique trunks or blanket chests can make great informal coffee tables. A tole, or thin metal, tray can be mounted on a stand to create a coffee table in a more formal setting. A basic Parsons table mixes well with many styles. Furniture designer Karl Springer was a master of the coffee table; he designed many during the 1970s.

CONSOLE TABLES are designed to fit against a wall. They can be simple or ornate. In the eighteenth century, an elaborately carved and gilded base was paired with a beautiful marble top. Today you might see a metal base with a glass top, or a table made entirely from wood. Console tables are often attached to the wall with brackets. Also typical are consoles that have curved, or demi-lune, fronts. There are also freestanding consoles with four legs. Console tables with a demi-lune front take up less space than a rectangular table. They are often used in pairs—on either side of a fireplace, for example. A single table could be centered on a wall in a front hall flanked by side chairs, or on a wall between two windows. A pier table is a variation of a console table, which is traditionally placed between two windows.

A **DROP-LEAF TABLE** has a center frame with two hinged flaps that drop down to conserve space. The gate-leg table, an early form of the drop-leaf table popular in seventeenth century England, has a leg that swings out, like a gate, to support the leaf. Drop-leaf tables can be used as both side tables and dining tables, making them perfect for small spaces. In a house with no dining room, a drop-leaf table can be placed against a wall in the kitchen or living room or a front hall and brought out for dining. A pair of side chairs flanking the table are attractive and useful.

A **DRUM TABLE** has a pedestal base and a circular top. Named for its resemblance to a drum, it is an English design first seen in the eighteenth century. A drum table is a relatively large piece of furniture and can be placed in either the center or the corner of a room. If a library, for example, has large proportions, the table can go in the center of the room. It often is made in mahogany with a leather top. It is a perfect place to stack books.

NESTING TABLES are a set of three or more tables of gradually decreasing size that fit under one another. They can be any style or material—from antique wood to stainless steel and glass. A nesting table is mostly used as a side table, with the option to use the smaller tables—for example, to eat dinner in front of the television.

A **PARSONS TABLE** has straight, square legs that are equal in width to the apron of the table. The furniture designer Jean-Michel Frank (1895–1941), who taught at the Paris branch of the Parsons School of Design in the 1930s, introduced his students to the table design. The students incorporated the design into their projects. When the students' work from Paris was exhibited in New York, local furniture makers began to reproduce the design, which was named the "Parsons table" and became widely used in the 1960s. A Parsons table can be made in any dimension and has a versatile and simple shape. Its clean lines enable it to mix well with most furniture. A Parsons table can be used as a coffee table, a side table, a dining table, or a desk—it's multipurpose. The form is such that it can be imaginatively and creatively finished. It can be lacquered or covered in fabric and painted or it can be stained wood.

PEDESTAL DINING TABLES have one or more pedestals, or center supports, depending on the length of the table. Having a pedestal on any dining table means no one gets stuck sitting next to a leg, which is convenient for seating. In some designs, leaves can be added for additional seating. This allows for greater flexibility as long as your dining room is large enough to fit the fully extended table. Pedestal dining tables date back to the eighteenth century, when houses began to have separate dining rooms. Before that, people sat at smaller tables throughout the house for their meals. Traditional pedestal dining tables are distinctly made for their purpose. You would put one only in a dining area. Recent designs are more versatile and could be used in less formal settings such as the kitchen or the corner of a living room.

A **PEMBROKE TABLE** is an eighteenth-century English design with a stationary center portion and hinged leaves. It usually has one or more drawers in the center of the front and either a pedestal or four legs. Supports for the leaves pull out from under the tabletop. It is thought that the first Pembroke table was designed in the mid- to late eighteenth century for the Earl of Pembroke. A Pembroke table is useful as a side table and can even be used for writing. Similar to the Pembroke table is the **sofa table**, which is an elongated version that is placed behind a sofa that is in the center of a room.

A **SIDEBOARD** is designed to go in a dining room to provide a surface for serving food and storage for silverware and table linens. It was a very popular piece of furniture in England in the eighteenth century. The English cabinetmakers George Hepplewhite and Thomas Sheraton designed sideboards, for example. There are also some particularly beautiful examples of antique sideboards from the Federal period in eighteenth-century America. There are also many styles that are more contemporary. The twentieth-century architect Frank Lloyd Wright designed side-boards, for example. A sideboard is an important piece of furniture, given its function, and therefore is very practical in a dining room.

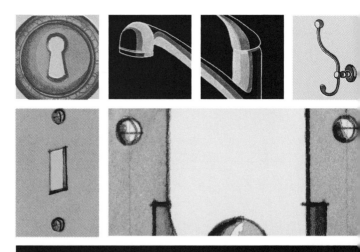

hardware

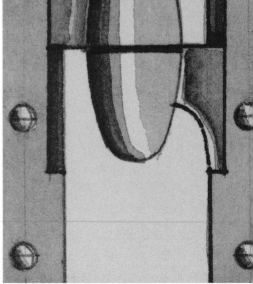

5

Hardware, such as door and cabinet knobs, hinges, and locks, is an important detail in decoration that should be given careful consideration. Suitable hardware will make a space look polished and finished. Restoring old hardware or selecting new hardware can be an effective facelift for a space.

There are many different finishes, from rustic wrought iron to sophisticated polished brass. Some hardware is ornate, which suits a traditional setting. Other styles of hardware have a streamlined design, which suits a contemporary setting. Many styles of reproduction hardware are available, and vintage hardware can be found in architectural salvage or antique shops. Ideally you want the finish and style of the hardware to be consistent throughout a house. The exception is hardware in kitchens and bathrooms. These rooms may vary from the rest of the house; however, there should be continuity within them, so that all hardware and fixtures, such as faucets and towel bars, coordinate.

Cabinet and Drawer Knobs

Available in an enormous variety of sizes, shapes, and finishes and easily installed, cabinet and drawer knobs are an opportunity to add a splash of color or a design element, especially in a kitchen or bathroom. The knob should be proportional to the piece it is on. You wouldn't want to put oversized knobs on a small cabinet door, for example. The knobs should also be suitable for the style and look of the room they are in. For a country kitchen that might mean iron or porcelain knobs. In a contemporary urban setting a simple chrome or nickel knob would be suitable. The alternative to cabinet knobs is cabinet pulls (see below).

Cabinet and Drawer Pulls

Cabinet and drawer pulls are handles, as opposed to knobs, used to open a cabinet or a drawer. Choosing pulls instead of knobs is purely a matter of taste. A pull will require drilling two holes instead of the one hole necessary for a knob. Pulls, or mounts as they are sometimes called when on antique forms of furniture, are typically made of metal and come in many finishes. Some fine antiques have exquisitely crafted pulls. Reproductions are available today and are suitable for drawers such as on an antique desk. For kitchen cabinets a simple stainless steel pull has a great contemporary look. Black iron pulls suit a country or Mediterranean look. The plate behind the pull, if there is one, is called an escutcheon plate.

Door Hardware

DOOR BUMPERS, or Doorstops, are used to prevent damage to a wall when a door is swung open. If a door is thrown open, the doorknob can go through the drywall or damage the plaster. There are a few different designs of door bumpers. Some models are installed directly onto the floor, others are installed on the wall at baseboard level directly below the doorknob. Illustrated is a doorstop installed on the wall at baseboard level.

DOORKNOBS come in a wide variety of materials from wood to glass to porcelain to metal. They can be round or oval or really any shape that is easily grabbed onto. Doorknobs often turn to operate a latch that secures the door. The latch mechanism that is traditionally used with a doorknob is called a mortise lock, which is set into the door. In recent years the less expensive and smaller tubular latch has become widely used. Some doors have dummy knobs, which are stationary and just pull a door open instead of latching the door in place. Doors with dummy knobs need a catch on the doorframe to help keep the door closed. A closet door might have a dummy knob or a pair of double doors, for example.

Lever Handles are an alternative to doorknobs. They come in a wide variety of styles and finishes. When your hands are full, it can be easier to open a door with lever handles as you don't have to twist a knob and can push it with your elbow or arm if need be. Lever handles come in right-hand and left-hand versions to suit doors that swing in different directions (whether the hinges are to the left or right). As with doorknobs, lever handles can be stationary, or dummy handles, or they can move to operate a latch.

HANDLE SETS are for exterior doors and have a deadbolt lock over the door handle. On the interior is a doorknob or a lever handle. The outside has a curved handle with a thumb latch, which you press down to open the door. The lock can either be a single-cylinder lock, which

requires a key only on the outside and a turn piece on the inside, or it can be a double-cylinder lock, which requires a key on both sides of the door. The finish of the handle set should match the hardware on the interior, if possible.

HINGES can be either a decorative detail or concealed for a cleaner look. They come in many finishes and, if visible, should be consistent with the hardware throughout the room. Below are a few frequently used hinges:

Butt Hinge is a standard hinge with two parts that meet, or butt, in the center. They come in a variety of sizes and finishes and it's important to check that you have the right hinge to hold the weight and size of the door you are hanging. The basic butt hinge can be dressed up with decorative finials if desired. There are a wide variety of choices in finials, too, from a plain square to a more elaborate urn shape.

A **Double-Action Hinge** allows the door to swing open in both directions. It is the hinge used for swinging doors, which are commonly seen in kitchens and dining rooms. This hinge is entirely functional and not decorative.

European Hinges, also called Concealed Hinges, are used mostly on cabinet doors. They are installed inside the door so that no hinge is visible, and they provide clean lines for cabinetwork.

H Hinges are decorative. With straight lines in an iron finish, they have an American Colonial or Mediterranean look. Simple H hinges are suitable in a rustic setting. Some H hinges are more elaborately designed and might have a polished brass finish, for example, lending a more sophisticated and dressier look than an iron H hinge.

HL Hinges are a variation of the H hinge. In iron they too can have an American Colonial look. The 'HL' part of the hinge will be visible on the side of the door that opens into a room. The finish should match the hardware in the rest of the room and, ideally, the house.

Olive Knuckle or **Bullet Hinges** are very attractive. When a door is closed, on the side of the door that opens inward you will see the bullet-shaped part of the hinge that is where the two parts meet and pivot. Bullet hinges have a classic look that is very versatile—they are a favorite.

Pivot Hinges are attached at the top and the bottom of a door—either a cabinet door or a full-sized door. They are less visible than standard butt hinges and are used frequently in contemporary design, especially on concealed doors, which are made to look like continuations of the wall—as if there were no door there at all.

Strap Hinges are typically made in iron and have a medieval look. Strap hinges were an early, rustic form of hinge. It's easy to imagine strap hinges on a battened oak door with iron studs at the entry to a fortress. A traditional decorative detail, they are also seen in American Colonial design on the interiors and exteriors of houses as well as on barn doors.

KEYHOLE PLATES, also known as Escutcheon Plates, are a metal surround for a keyhole. Escutcheon means a protective plate and applies to other hardware applications, such as the push plates used for swinging doors. Keyhole plates are typically used on doors with mortise locks, which is a type of latch or locking mechanism installed into a door. Keyhole plates are also seen on cabinetwork such as an armoire or any cupboard that locks. Like all hardware, they

come in a wide variety of styles and finishes and should match the other hardware in the room. Some are elaborately ornamented.

LOCKS AND BOLTS are essential to the security of a house and to privacy within it. It's a good idea to change the locks on exterior doors after moving to a new house, and if you are doing renovation work, wait until the work is finished to change the locks. For convenience you may wish to have all exterior locks keyed alike, so they use the same key, and a locksmith can easily do this for you. A deadbolt is the most standard and time-tested form of security for an exterior door. You will also see newer combination locks or digital locks that do not require a key.

A **Cremone Bolt** is an elegant, ornate, and decorative surface-mounted bolt typically seen on a French door. It runs the height of the door and its handle is turned to extend the bolt into the doorframe and the threshold or the floor. The more contemporary alternative to a cremone bolt is a simpler surface-mounted bolt.

Cylinder Locks, found on exterior doors, have a deadbolt and are widely used. A double-cylinder lock requires a key on both the inside and the outside of the door, while a single-cylinder lock uses a key just on the outside and a thumb-turn, a piece you manually turn to operate the lock, on the inside. With a single-cylinder lock, a burglar could conceivably break sidelights or a window in the door, reach through, and unlock the door. On the other hand, a double-cylinder lock can be dangerous in a fire because you need a key to unlock the door from the interior. If you have a double-cylinder lock, be sure to keep the key in a safe place.

Mortise Locks are installed into the edge of a door so they are not visible when the door is closed. Because they have to be cut into a door, the door must have a certain thickness. The word "mortise" means a hole cut into a piece of wood. Mortise locks are the classic lockset. Today, they are most frequently used on entry doors, though it's also very nice to use them on interior doors. They come either with deadbolts for entry doors or with privacy locks or just basic latches for interior doors. Historically, mortise locks were used on all doors throughout a house. Today, the less expensive tubular latch is more widely seen on interior doors. Mortise locks have a historic look. They are generally more durable than a tubular latch.

A **Privacy Lock** is a button in the center of a doorknob that can be pushed or twisted to lock the knob. It is used primarily in a bathroom or a bedroom to prevent someone from opening the door. It should not be used as a primary means of securing a house. Privacy locks can have an emergency release, which allows the door to be unlocked from the outside using a piece of wire. This is a good safety option to consider, especially if you have children who might lock themselves in a bathroom.

Rim Locks, or **Box Locks**, were used in eighteenth-century England, Europe, and America but not manufactured in America until the mid-nineteenth century. They are made of metal—brass and iron are typical—and mounted onto the surface of a door. They can come with a deadbolt for an entrance door or with lighter locks for interior doors. Their traditional, historic architectural look can be either rustic or sophisticated and can complement an older house or apartment. Rim locks are made for both right-hand and left-hand doors. The direction of the door opening will determine which one you need. They can also be used on double doors.

Surface Bolts affix to a door and have a bolt that slides into the doorframe at the top or into the floor or threshold at the bottom. They are good looking and are often seen on double doors and French doors. Most surface bolts are installed vertically. On double doors or French doors, you can use a bolt at the top of each door and a bolt at the bottom of each door. Since they are operable only from the inside, do not use these locks on a primary entrance door. Surface bolts come in different sizes and finishes; smaller ones, called **slide bolts**, can be installed horizontally. They go just above or below a doorknob as a privacy lock for a bathroom or a bedroom. A fancier version of the surface bolt is called a cremone bolt (see page 130), which was traditionally used on French doors.

A **Tubular Latch** is a mechanism that holds a door closed, operated by a doorknob or a door handle. It is very widely used today, while historically, doors on the interior of a house had mortise locks, which are larger, more expensive, and more durable. But today most doors come predrilled for tubular latches.

PUSH PLATES are installed onto swinging doors about 4 feet from the floor to prevent fingerprints on the door itself. The plate can be metal, glass, or a synthetic, such as Plexiglas. Glass or clear synthetics are the least obvious, though glass can crack. A simple stainless steel push plate is quite attractive and has a twentieth-century look to it. For a more historic look, try a brass push plate with decorative detail.

Hardware Finishes

Hardware finishes will help to set the tone of the style of a room. Generally, the finish on hardware should be consistent throughout a house. The exception is kitchens and bathrooms, which can have a different hardware finish from the rest of the house. Polished brass is dressier than wrought iron. Bronze has a wonderful warm color. Chrome is known to be durable and to resist corrosion, making it a popular choice for kitchens and bathrooms. Nickel has been widely used in contemporary design and has a great soft, silvery color. Stainless steel has a modern look and is very durable. Some finishes can be "oiled," giving them a darker, richer color that can be very attractive and versatile. Some finishes, such as brass, may tarnish or pit unless coated to prevent this. When shopping for hardware, it's a good idea to ask about specific finishes and how they will stand up over time.

BRASS is an alloy of copper and zinc. It can be polished to a high shine or antiqued to have an older look. To prevent tarnishing, brass can be lacquered, or it can be left unlacquered to age through oxidization. If brass is not lacquered, it will have to be polished regularly to keep it shiny. Although lacquering will extend the polished effect, it will show scratches over time. Brass is a versatile finish that can be used in traditional or contemporary settings. In eighteenth-century England it was kept highly polished, which took a good amount of effort. Today lacquer makes possible a low-maintenance polished look.

BRONZE is an alloy of copper and tin, sometimes mixed with other metals. It has a deep warm color and develops a beautiful patina over time. Bronze has a low luster matte finish, quite unlike bright and shiny polished brass. Gilded bronze is called ormolu and is often seen on fine antiques. There are also versatile oil-rubbed bronze finishes that are a rich brown and do not tarnish.

CHROME FINISH is a plating of chromium over another metal, most often brass. Polished chrome has a bright silvery look with a cool bluish tint. A satin chrome finish is matte silver. Chrome has a modern, twentieth-century look. Chrome will not tarnish and is resistant to corrosion. It is an ideal finish for utilitarian spaces such as kitchens and bathrooms and also can be used throughout the house.

IRON can either be wrought or cast. Stainless steel, mentioned below, is also made with iron.

Cast Iron has a higher carbon content and is more brittle than wrought iron. It can be cast into complex shapes. In the early eighteenth century, English ironmaster Abraham Darcy began to smelt iron using coke instead of coal, an improvement to iron production that led to the mass production of cast iron as a building material.

A historic combination is oak and iron; it was seen in the Tudor period of the sixteenth century, for example. Iron is widely used for decorative details from doorknobs to the handrail on a staircase. It can be waxed to help prevent rusting.

Wrought Iron is traditionally hammered and twisted into shape by the blacksmith while the iron is hot. It has a very low carbon content, which makes it relatively soft and malleable. It is still possible to find handmade wrought iron, as well as more technologically modern versions of the old technique. A wrought-iron finish has a rustic look that is suitable in country, Mediterranean, or Southwestern styles, for example.

NICKEL is a metallic element with a silvery color that can have a polished or a matte finish, which is also called satin or brushed. Nickel has a beautiful soft gray color that is warmer than chrome, which tends to go a little blue. It is a finish that has been widely used in contemporary design. Nickel does not tarnish.

ORMOLU is gilded bronze that was often found on French furniture and decorative objects, such as candlesticks, during the seventeenth and eighteenth centuries. Motifs, moldings, handles, and mounts, or pulls, were made of ormolu. The gilding lends a very sophisticated look that is often ornate. Ormolu does not tarnish.

PORCELAIN is a decorative finish that can be glazed with a design or left plain. The types of hardware made of porcelain are mostly doorknobs and cabinet and drawer knobs. Porcelain is not as practical as metal as it can chip and crack—as any ceramic does. It is pretty, however, to have blue and white porcelain knobs in a country bedroom.

STAINLESS STEEL is iron alloyed with 10 to 20 percent chromium, which prevents corrosion. It is often used for the hardware on boats, but is also very attractive for residential use. It has a twentieth-century look. There are some particularly attractive kitchen cabinet and drawer hardware made of it. Stainless steel will not tarnish.

Hooks

Hooks are a great item for keeping things neat and saving space. A double hook has two prongs and a single hook has one. The hooks themselves can be small for dishtowels in the kitchen or larger for heavy coats in a mudroom. Putting hooks in a closet adds to the usable space, and on the back of a bathroom door they allow for an extra towel or bathrobe.

Kitchen and Bathroom Hardware

FAUCETS come in many designs. The look depends on the finish and the style. Some are highly ornate, gilded faucets, and others are basic utilitarian designs. Faucets can have cross handles or lever handles. Deciding between the two is a matter of preference. Illustrated here is a cross-handle faucet.

Lever-Handle Faucet is an alternative to a cross-handle faucet. It's a matter of personal preference what you choose. The finish and design of the faucet and spout determine their style.

Single-Lever Faucet is one lever that operates the hot and the cold water as well as the water pressure. This is great for a kitchen faucet.

SPOUTS for sinks can have a low profile, meaning they are essentially straight, or a gooseneck profile, meaning they are arched. There are even highly ornate spouts shaped like animal heads where water rushes from the mouth. A basic utilitarian straight spout, which is illustrated here, has a low profile and will suit most situations.

A **Gooseneck Spout** is very useful and can be great in a kitchen or laundry room. Some people prefer a gooseneck spout, which has an old-fashioned feel, as it makes it easier to wash a big pot — or a small dog — in the sink.

Rosettes

Rosettes are circular plates that are flush with a door, wall, or drawer behind a doorknob, lever handle, drawer pull, or hook, for example. A rosette is also a type of round trimming decorated like a flower. A rosette should complement whatever it goes behind, and the finish and design should be the same.

Switch Plates

Switch plates cover the area around light switches. Related are outlet covers, which cover the area around electrical outlets, and cable covers, which cover the area around cable wires. All of these are made in different dimensions to cover one, two, or more switches or outlets. It is best if all of these are as unobtrusive as possible. They can be painted to match the wall, and if the room is wallpapered, the plates can be covered in paper.

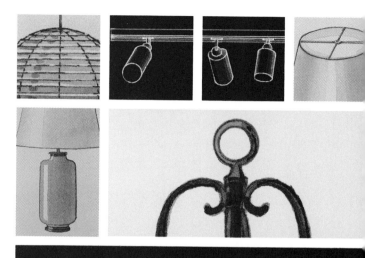

lighting

6

Good lighting is essential to a comfortable house. Achieving the right combination of primary and background lighting takes some planning. Primary, or direct light, is important for reading, working in the kitchen, or at a desk. Background lighting is for atmosphere and to fill a room with light. ■ Most rooms should have a combination of primary and background lighting. In some rooms, such as hallways and dining rooms, background lighting alone can be sufficient. When designing a house, it's important to think in advance about where you want to read and work, and to plan accordingly. If you're doing construction or renovating, plan the lighting early so wiring can be run for ceiling and wall fixtures and so that outlets and switches are placed conveniently. ■ Lighting technology is developing quickly, and in addition to the standard types of bulbs—incandescent, fluorescent, and halogen—there are now alternatives such as fiber optic lighting.

Bulbs

FLUORESCENT BULBS, introduced in the 1930s, produce light by passing an electrical current through a gas-filled tube. They are more expensive than incandescent bulbs but last much longer and use less electricity. This is why most office buildings use them. The color of the light is cooler and, some might say, harsher than light from an incandescent bulb. However, warm white fluorescent bulbs, which soften the light considerably, are available. Fluorescent bulbs typically are long tubes that fit into a ballast, which can be mounted onto a ceiling or under cabinets, for example. There are also compact fluorescent bulbs that fit into an incandescent base. Since fluorescent bulbs are more energy efficient and now come in warmer white, they should be considered for utilitarian areas in a house.

HALOGEN BULBS, filled with a gas of "halogens," burn very bright and have a long life. Their light shines crisper and brighter white than that of an incandescent bulb. Because halogen bulbs burn very hot, they should not be used in areas where people might bump into them or near flammable items. Halogen lights are best in areas where you want primary direct lighting, such as above a desk or countertop or in a bathroom.

INCANDESCENT is the most common type of bulb. They are inexpensive, easy to find, and the standard bulb most lamps are fitted for. Incandescent means glowing with heat, which is what the filament in the bulb does. The invention of the incandescent bulb was a major historic turning point, making possible the transition from candles and gas lamps to electric lamps for light.

In the early nineteenth century it was discovered that light could be produced by running electricity through a filament. The big question was what type of filament would not burn out quickly. It wasn't until 1879 that American inventor Thomas Edison developed a bulb that lasted more than a few hours. This bulb had a carbon-coated bamboo filament. In the early 1900s General Electric developed a tungsten filament, which is still used today. The downside of incandescent bulbs is that they burn most of the electricity they use as heat and are therefore more wasteful than other bulbs. They can be tinted; pink bulbs have a soft, warm light that is great in any room. Bulbs come in a few sizes, regular and small, called candle bulbs, which are often used in wall sconces.

Ceiling Fixtures

Ceiling fixtures require an electrical source in the ceiling. In some ceilings there is an existing electrical box covered by a cap; otherwise, a hole will have to be cut into the ceiling to find an electrical line. This isn't major construction but will require some repair and repainting. If you are building or renovating, consider early where you might want an electrical box in the ceiling. The box should be connected to a wall switch that will operate the ceiling fixture. A dimmer, which allows you to adjust the brightness of the light, is always a good idea.

A **CANOPY AND CHAIN** are needed to hang most lighting fixtures from the ceiling. The canopy is a convex cap that covers the electric box in the ceiling. The chain is what the fixture hangs from. The length of the chain determines how low the fixture will hang. There should be at least 6 feet, 8 inches of clearance from the floor to the bottom of the fixture, unless the fixture is over a table, in which case there should be approximately 3 feet between the tabletop and the bottom of the fixture. Many fixtures come with a canopy and chain in a complementary style. It's a good idea when buying a ceiling fixture to ask if the canopy and chain are included.

CHANDELIER is a lighting fixture that hangs from the ceiling. Before the age of electric light-bulbs, the candles on a chandelier had to be changed frequently, so chandeliers were attached to a pulley system that allowed them to be lowered. Chandeliers historically were found only in the grandest of houses and even then would have been lighted only on special occasions. Chandeliers can be very fancy, adorned with crystal or cut glass to reflect the light. A metal chandelier, of brass, iron, or tole, gives a less formal look. Chandeliers have a luxurious sensibility. One thinks of them over the table in a formal dining room or as a focal point in a living room or entry hall. In a large space, a chandelier can visually pull the room together. It is very important that the size of the chandelier be proportional to the room. You wouldn't want to put a small chandelier in the center of a large room as it would look dinky. Conversely, a large chandelier in a small space will take over the room.

COVE LIGHTING is installed on a wall behind a concave molding that conceals the fixtures but allows light to shine upward onto the ceiling. It is usually installed around the top portion of a wall but can also be installed into a ceiling. Cove lighting has a modern look—it is often seen in Art Deco design—and it can be used in conjunction with recessed or track lighting on the ceiling. The lights should be on a dimmer to create ambiance. Cove lighting is an architectural detail, meaning that it is a built-in part of the structure and not a fixture that is quickly changed.

LANTERNS are decorative cases, often of glass with a metal frame, that are used to protect an open flame. Lanterns have been used for centuries to light interior and exterior spaces such as hallways and entrances. Besides hanging from the ceiling, a lantern can be affixed to a wall or even placed on a tabletop. Lanterns in general are a good source of background lighting. There are many styles; two favorites are:

Hall Lanterns are made with brass or iron and glass. They can be used successfully in an entry hall, outside a front or back door, or over a staircase. Many styles of hall lanterns are reproduced today, and older ones can be found at antique stores or flea markets. The look is suitable for a house in the country or a city apartment—it is timeless and versatile.

Paper Lanterns emit a soft glow that can be quite beautiful. They are most commonly white paper globes that hang from the ceiling, although they are sometimes made with colored paper. The design is originally Asian. Paper lanterns in the form of standing lamps, table lamps, or even wall fixtures can be found. They have the typical rich simplicity of a Japanese look and can suit a wide variety of situations, from a dorm room to a kitchen to an elegant dining room, depending on the style of the lamp. The light from a paper lantern is generally muted and provides background lighting. In the 1950s, the landscape and furniture designer Isamu Noguchi (1904–1988) designed great paper lanterns that are still made today. In paper and bamboo, they are a fusion of traditional Japanese and modern design. Some of the Noguchi lamps hang from floor to ceiling and can look great in an alcove or corner. They are quite sculptural and make an interesting addition to a room.

A **PENDANT FIXTURE** hangs from the ceiling. There are many varieties, and they can be hung alone or in a series. A pendant, sometimes called a Hanging Fixture, can provide both background and primary lighting. Some styles have a globe that provides diffused background lighting, and others shine light directly onto a work surface for primary lighting. Pendant fixtures are a less formal and more contemporary alternative to a chandelier. In contemporary design you will sometimes see a series of small pendant lights installed above a countertop in a kitchen. This can look attractive and provides abundant light. It's always a good idea to put ceiling light fixtures on a wall switch with a dimmer.

RECESSED LIGHTING has fixtures, called cans, recessed into the ceiling. Recessed lights come with a choice of trims, some of which diffuse light for background lighting, some that direct the light for an accent, and some that are wall washers, which will bathe a wall, or area, in light. An accent light might be used to highlight a piece of art, while a wall washer will throw light in a broader area to highlight a wall hanging, for example. You can vary the trim from can to can to have a combination of functions. Recessed lighting has a clean contemporary look that can be used in any setting. While recessed lighting is not typical of traditional design, it is such an unobtrusive and convenient way to light a room that it can work in a traditional setting. Visually, recessed lighting is preferable to track lighting, but track lighting is much more flexible as you can swivel the fixtures and add lamps if need be. Before installing recessed lighting, make sure your furniture plan is final and place the lights accordingly because you won't be able to move them once they're installed. If you have a concrete ceiling, which cans cannot be recessed into, and you want to install recessed lighting, then a new ceiling must be built at a lower level that creates enough space for the cans to fit up into. This is called a dropped ceiling. Otherwise, you will have to use surface-mounted fixtures or track lighting. The minimum can depth is 5 to 6 inches. These lights should be on dimmers for maximum flexibility.

SURFACE MOUNT is a general term for a fixture that is directly mounted on the ceiling. There are many different styles of surface-mounted lighting, from the generic overhead lights seen in bathrooms, closets, and kitchens to more ornate and elaborate styles for living rooms or dining rooms. Many surface-mount fixtures hold up to three or four bulbs and generate quite a lot of background lighting. In a room with low ceilings, a surface-mounted fixture is preferable to a hanging fixture. The fixture should be centered on the ceiling, and it's always a good idea to have a dimmer on the wall.

TRACK LIGHTING consists of a series of separate lamps that fit into a metal track secured to the ceiling. Track lighting has a twentieth-century look. The lamps can swivel, more can be added if needed, and the size of the lamps can vary. When installing track lighting, take some time to think about the track placement. The lamps can be moved on the track, but the track itself cannot easily be moved once installed. Also, finalize the furniture layout and design of the room to make sure there will be light where you need it — such as over a kitchen counter and a breakfast table. A track can be a straight line or it can be shaped like an H, or a U, or an L. Compared to recessed lighting, track lighting is less subtle to look at but allows for more flexibility and easier installation.

Dimmers

A dimmer, also called a rheostat, controls the brightness of the bulb. A dimmer can be either on a wall switch or installed directly onto a lamp. In general, all ceiling and wall fixtures are best installed so they turn on and off using a wall switch with a dimmer. It's important to be able to dim the lights to create ambiance in any room. A room with bright lights is not conducive to a relaxing dinner, for example. For anything but a reading lamp, a dimmer is very useful. Dimmers can always be added; it is an easy installation.

Display Lighting

Display lighting is an important consideration and can take a few different forms. The traditional reflector light over a painting is one form of display lighting. Small concealed strips of lights can be installed inside of a cabinet. This is an effective way to light a cabinet and is a good idea if you have decorative objects in it. You will of course need an electrical source near the cabinet for this purpose.

Tole

Tole is sheet metal that is often painted and sometimes gilded. Tole was traditionally used for lampshades and lighting fixtures as it isn't flammable. Decorative objects such as trays are also made from tole. The look of it is quite varied, from rustic to formal, depending on how it's finished. Since tole is often painted, it can be quite colorful and decorative. A bouillotte table lamp always has a tole lampshade.

WALL-MOUNTED DISPLAY FIXTURES are installed on the wall over a built-in bookcase or cabinet and are wired directly into the bookcase or wall. They are more suited to built-in shelving than to a freestanding piece of furniture. Unlike other types of display lighting, the fixtures are visible and become a part of the overall design of the room. These types of fixtures are seen often in contemporary design, but suit any look, including traditional. The finish of the fixtures should match or be similar to other hardware in the room. It's best if these lights are on dimmers to create ambiance in the evenings.

Lampshades

Lampshades have the practical purpose of muting the direct glare of a bulb. While all detail in decorating is important, lampshades in particular can make a big difference. It is important to scale the shade correctly to the lamp. A good lampshade, while not that expensive, can help to finish a room, but don't go overboard. Having too many lampshades in a room can distract the eye from the overall design. Smaller clip-on shades for wall sconces are much less distracting.

FABRIC LAMPSHADES are more formal than paper lampshades. They can be made of fabric stretched over a frame, with a knife or box pleat, or with shirred fabric. Stretched fabric shades used to be in vogue, but now pleated shades are more popular. The fabric can be anything from lightweight cotton to textured linen to silk. Fabric shades are more flexible than paper shades—they can be designed in many different shapes. Dark fabric lets less light through.

Custom-made shades allow for the most choice, but tape, fringe, or gimp trimmings can be applied to jazz up a ready-made shade. If trimmings are sewn on, then it is possible to hand wash the shade. If they are glued on, the glue will not stand up to washing.

White or off-white fabric shades will look warmer and softer if they have a pale pink lining. If budget permits, a custom-made, stretched silk velvet lampshade is chic.

PAPER LAMPSHADES can be made in many colors and tend to be less formal than fabric shades. Translucent paper shades allow a lot of light to shine through and are best for reading, bedside, or desk lamps. Opaque paper shades are better for lamps used for background lighting, such as in a hallway or on a standing lamp in a corner. Generally speaking, paper shades are more contemporary looking and understated than fabric shades. The rolled edge of a paper shade can be done in a contrasting colored paper, which adds a great detail. In rooms with a dark wall color, dark lampshades, such as green, red, or even black, can look very chic.

Scaling a Lampshade

Scaling a lampshade is an art. A well-scaled lampshade complements the lamp it is on, rather than appearing too big or too small.

Lampshades have three measurements: the diameter of the top, the slant between the top and bottom, and the diameter of the bottom. The measurements are usually given in that order. A 9-by-12-by-17-inch lampshade, for example, is a standard size.

A lampshade mutes the glare of the bulb and hides the fixture. The right size and shape for a lampshade depends on the lamp, but there are some general guidelines. On a standing lamp, use a slightly bigger shade that covers the very top of the body of the lamp. This will help to hide the fixture when people are looking up at the lamp. On a table lamp or a lamp that people look down at, the shade can stop an inch or less above the body, so the neck of the lamp is just visible. It is best when you can just see the neck of the lamp.

Lampshade Details

CLIP-ON LAMPSHADES clip directly onto the bulb and are used with lamps that do not have harps. Clip-on shades are made both for a regular size bulb and for smaller candle bulbs, which are generally seen in wall sconces. There are clip-on attachments available for lampshades with a washer fitting.

The **HARP** is the oblong metal piece on a lamp that a washer-fitted lampshade is secured to. The harp is fitted into the socket of the lamp. Harps come in different sizes—from approximately 6 to 12 inches high or more. A lampshade should be scaled to the size of the lamp then, accordingly, a harp is chosen that will put the lampshade at the correct height. A socket on a lamp is either harp-fitting or not. If the socket can't hold a harp, then you need to use a clip-on lampshade. It also is possible to remove a harp so that a clip-on shade can be used.

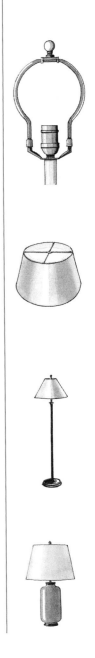

Lampshades with a **WASHER FITTING** have a ring at the center of the top of the shade that fits onto the harp and is secured with a finial. An adapter can be attached to a washer-fitting lampshade so that it clips directly onto the bulb.

Standing Lamps

Standing lamps stand on the floor instead of, for example, on a table like a table lamp. The design is good for tight spaces, especially where there may not be room for a table. A standing lamp positioned just behind a chair or at the end of a sofa will make a good reading lamp. There are styles that have a small shelf built around the pole, which makes a useful surface for putting a drink on.

Table Lamps

Table lamps are probably the most common form of lighting. Almost every room has at least one or two table lamps. They are typically found on either side of a bed and on side tables in the living room or library. Keep in mind that too many lampshades in a room can be distracting, so alternative lighting sources such as ceiling or wall fixtures should be considered. There is a table lamp for every look and style. Some common shapes of bases are a candlestick, an urn, and a sphere.

BOUILLOTTE is a French-style lamp that was named after a card game popular in the nineteenth century. It traditionally has a dish at the base to hold the game pieces, a metal shade, and candle brackets. The height of the candle brackets is adjustable so they can be raised as the candles burn down. Stylish and timeless, bouillottes are great desk lamps and work well in a library.

GOOSENECK LAMPS are the best lamps for a desk. They have a long, curved neck so that light shines directly onto a surface. The gooseneck shape is also seen on standing lamps.

Uplights

Uplights project light up toward the ceiling. They can be tall like a standing lamp or as small and low as a can that sits on the floor. Tall uplights are also called torchères. In the corner of a room an uplight illuminates a ceiling. It can be used to add to the background lighting and to the variety of light sources in the room.

Wall Fixtures

WALL-MOUNTED LAMPS are affixed to the wall. They can have a stationary arm or a swing-arm that is jointed. Wall-mounted lamps come in a variety of finishes, including chrome, iron, brass, or even a gilded finish. They always have a lampshade that can be paper, fabric, or tole. One of the best-known styles, the Hansen Lamp, was designed by George Hansen. Ideal places for a wall-mounted lamp are next to a bed or over a comfortable reading chair. They are great in tight spaces where there isn't enough room for a table and table lamp. Wall-mounted lamps can be wired directly into the wall or have a cord (under a cord cover) running down the wall to an outlet at floor level. If you're not sure what your furniture placement will be, it's a good idea to use a cord cover and plug the lamp in at the baseboard. This allows for more flexibility than having the lamp wired directly into the wall. For bedside use, the lamps should be mounted approximately 42 inches off the floor.

WALL SCONCES are light fixtures mounted on a wall about 5 to 6 feet off the floor, depending on the ceiling height. They are functional as well as decorative. Early wall sconces were less decorative and more just a means to support candles on the wall, but, starting in approximately the eighteenth century when the decorative arts were flourishing, some elaborately designed sconces were seen. Today sconces can still hold candles, but are often electrified and have candle bulbs, small incandescent bulbs designed to look like candles. They can be either modern or traditional depending on the finish and design. A gilded and carved wooden sconce is traditional and formal, while a sconce with a chrome finish and few decorative details is more contemporary looking. Sconces are excellent on either side of a fireplace, in dining rooms, and in halls. They should be used for background, not primary, lighting. Sconces have one or multiple arms—the more arms, the more light. If possible, wall sconces should be put on a dimmer to control the light level in the room, for ambiance and atmosphere. They can have small clip-on lampshades to mute the glare of the bulbs; if they don't have lampshades they must be on a dimmer. Wall sconces should be wired directly into a wall.

motifs

7

Motifs are the patterns and designs that appear
again and again on architecture, furniture, wallpapers,
and fabrics. They can be used as a single image,
perhaps painted in the center of a table, or they
can be repeated to form borders on walls or furniture. They are even seen in corporate logos.
Certain motifs have become typical of particular
cultures: in ancient Egypt images of the scarab and
the lotus were often replicated; in the Pennsylvania
Dutch area of the United States, hex signs are seen
on the sides of barns; and in the Southwest you
frequently see Native American images such as the
dancing man, Kokopelli. This chapter focuses on
motifs that have endured through the ages.

Motif Types

ACANTHUS LEAVES are spiny, textured leaves that were first used as ornament by the Greeks. The Romans also used the acanthus leaf widely in architectural decoration. The acanthus plant is native to the Mediterranean region.

ARABESQUE is an ornamental motif with spiraling, intertwined vines and leaves. It was widely used in Islamic art as well as on painted furniture from the fifteenth century to the present. It is presumably a derivation of the tree of life motif (see page 157). You are likely to see the arabesque motif on carpets, fabrics, and plaster work. A painted arabesque on a cabinet, chest, or wall can look very pretty.

BEAD AND REEL MOTIF is a string of oval shapes alternating with round shapes. It is used widely in Classical architecture, especially on narrow moldings in the entablature—the area above the columns that has a cornice, frieze, and architrave. The bead and reel motif is also used as a detail on furniture.

A **CARTOUCHE** has a smooth central surface surrounded by scroll-like carvings. Sometimes words are carved into the flat surface area. It is used frequently in Classical architecture and is seen on the exterior of many buildings today. The word cartouche is derived from the Italian *cartoccio*, meaning a roll of paper. A cartouche is often centered over a doorway on the exterior of a building.

CHEVRON is a V-shaped motif that, when run in a series, forms a zigzag or herringbone pattern. The chevron motif has been used from Roman times to the present. It is seen today as the logo at Chevron gas stations. Patterns such as the chevron or herringbone add subtle detail and interest and can be incorporated in a fabric design or a wood floor, for example.

EGG AND DART is a Classical Greek motif. It is designed to fit into a quarter-round of molding and looks like a series of eggs with their tops cut off that are separated by pointed shapes, or darts. Classical architecture often has egg and dart, or a variation of it, on the capitals, or top, of columns. Today, you might also see the egg and dart motif on crown moldings or as a detail carved into the edge of a table. This pattern works best when carved into relief.

FLEUR-DE-LIS is a delicate motif used by French royalty as far back as the twelfth century. It depicts three petals of an iris flower tied with a band. Symbolizing royalty, the fleur-de-lis is often used on porcelain, fabrics, and ironwork. You are also likely to see this motif in metalwork and business logos.

GREEK KEY is a geometrical design that is often the basis of fretwork, which is an ornamental band seen in architecture and on furniture. The Greek key, as might be suspected, is originally Greek and has many variations. It is often used as detail on the interiors and exteriors of buildings.

The **HONEYSUCKLE MOTIF**, also called Anthemion, is originally Greek and has a few variations. *Anthemion* is the Greek word for "flower." Honeysuckle is a shrub with a fragrant flower that grows in many locations around the world. The honeysuckle motif was seen frequently in the late eighteenth century and early nineteenth century during the Neoclassical period as an ornament on furniture and decorative objects.

LINENFOLD MOTIF shows folded cloth. It was widely seen in Gothic architecture, and is thought to symbolize the cloth used during Mass.

The linenfold motif lends itself to being carved in relief and is seen mostly on wooden panels.

The **LOTUS MOTIF** was used by the ancient Egyptians and Greeks as well as by many Asian cultures. The Buddha is frequently shown seated on a lotus flower, which is a symbol of compassion and purity. The lotus flower represents purity because it can grow in muddy water yet produce a beautiful clean flower. The Egyptians used the lotus motif on the capitals of their columns. It was popular during the Art Deco period in the early twentieth century, and therefore you might see it in the South Beach section of Miami, where the Art Deco style has been well preserved.

LOZENGE is a diamond-shaped motif, geometrically defined as an equilateral shape with two acute angles and two obtuse angles—which means that it's a slightly oblong diamond. Historically the diamond was used on shields, banners, and furniture. On the exterior of buildings, you will sometimes see the lozenge used as an ornamental detail. An all-over pattern with diamonds in alternating colors is suitable for a painted floor.

QUATREFOIL is a motif shaped like a four-leaf clover. It is typical of Gothic architecture, appearing at least since the twelfth century in Europe and is often seen inside and outside churches and cathedrals. It is sometimes, but not always, enclosed inside a circle. The word *foil* refers to the leaves in the pattern and *quatre* is "four" in French. A cinquefoil has five leaves and a trefoil has three leaves. St. Patrick's Cathedral in New York City has many quatrefoils as architectural details on the exterior.

A **SHELL MOTIF** was widely seen in the Rococo period, which flourished in France during the early eighteenth century. Italian grottoes of old often had walls embedded with shells, and an eighteenth-century shell mania made it trendy to adorn furniture and walls with them. On chairs with cabriole legs, you sometimes see a shell carved into the knee. Today, like the chevron, the shell motif is used as a major gas company's logo.

SINGERIE is a monkey motif. The word *singe* means "monkey" in French. In the late seventeenth century the artist Jean Berain began to depict monkeys dressed as humans frolicking. Berain was appointed Dessinateur de la Chambre et du Cabinet du Roi (Designer of the King's Living Quarters) by King Louis XIV of France in 1674, and singerie became popular. Decorating a room with a theme such as monkeys or zebras or tigers is an amusing idea that will certainly create a conversation piece.

The **TREE OF LIFE MOTIF** depicts a curving tree with swirling branches and leaves. It has been used for thousands of years and has been adapted by many different cultures. The paisley pattern, for example, is thought to be an offshoot of the tree of life. Palampores are beautiful panels of fabric painted or printed with a tree of life. It is likely that the arabesque is also derived from it. The twentieth-century architect Frank Lloyd Wright designed stained glass windows using a modern take on this ancient motif.

URN MOTIF shows a decorative vase. It was seen widely in Greek architecture and design. Originally used to hold the remains of a cremated body, urns eventually were depicted as decorative detail. During the Neoclassical period in the late eighteenth and early nineteenth centuries, the urn motif was often repeated. Scottish architect Robert Adam frequently used the urn motif during that period. Today you see the shape in many places — from finials to the base of a lamp.

trimmings

8

Trimmings add a finishing touch to curtains, upholstered furniture, lampshades, and soft-goods such as bedskirts, bedspreads, throw pillows, and tablecloths. One function of trimmings is to cover unsightly seams. They can also add a sense of drama or fun to a room—bullion fringe can be quite dramatic, while ball fringe is quite playful. Store-bought items can be spruced up with gimp, tape, or fringe. Trimmings should suit the look of the room. Silk fringe is more formal than cotton fringe, for example. Trimmings can be custom-made for a perfect color match, but there is a wide selection of ready-made trimmings available. You will sometimes see trimmings referred to by the French term *passementerie.*

Trimming Types

CORD is a round, twisted, or braided trimming that is either sewn into or over a seam or glued over a seam. Cord must be attached to a piece of fabric tape to be sewn into a seam. Cord is used to trim upholstered furniture such as a sofa, chair, or bench. You also use it to trim curtains and headboards, throw pillows, and bedskirts. On a bedskirt or a sofa or chair skirt, an elegant upholstery detail is to use cord to trim the seam at the top of the skirt and tape along the bottom of the skirt, closest to the floor. A less dressy alternative to cord is piping and welting, which is basic cording covered in fabric. A self-welt is cording covered in the primary upholstery fabric.

CORD AND TASSEL is a twisted cord with a decorative tassel at the end. Thick cord with sizable tassels is used to make elegant tie-backs for important curtains. Smaller cord and tassels can be used on a loose seat cushion if the cord is set into the seam of the cushion and extends beyond the cushion to tie onto the back of the chair. You can even place the smallest cord and tassel on the key to a cabinet or chest.

FRINGE adds a touch of elegance. It is a trimming in which yarn, tassels, or even wooden beads hang from a band or tape. It can be sewn into fabric seams or applied on top of a seam. The threads of the fringe can be cut or looped; it is a matter of personal taste. Fringe can match the fabric it is trimming, or it can bring out colors elsewhere in the room. A heavier fringe should be used with heavier fabrics or on larger pieces, and a more delicate fringe on more delicate pieces. For curtains, valances, lampshades, throw pillows, tablecloths, and upholstered furniture, fringe can be a great addition. Some particular types of fringe are:

Ball Fringe has little fluffy balls hanging on a tape. It can be whimsical and fun; you might use it on country curtains or a bedspread. It is generally made of cotton and not too dressy.

Bullion Fringe is a heavy fringe that is 6 to 9 inches long and used at the bottom of upholstery instead of a skirt. This type of fringe evokes a period look and can be quite dramatic. It gives a room elegance. It can be one color or multicolored.

Molded Fringe is made from wooden turnings, or beads, that are elaborately adorned with multicolored threads. The drops can be many different shapes—some long, some round. This was a popular trimming in the eighteenth and nineteenth centuries, when it was used primarily for curtains and valances. It is still seen today in period rooms.

Tassel Fringe is made with tassels that are evenly spaced or in clusters. The tassels can be all one size or varying sizes, one color or multicolored. Tassel fringe is used primarily on curtains, valances, throw pillows, or around the bottoms of lampshades.

GIMP is a braid used as trim on furniture with a wooden frame. The French spelling *guimpe* is frequently used. Gimp is glued down to cover the upholstery tacks where the fabric meets the wood. Nail heads can also be used for this purpose. Gimp has a pretty, decorative quality and is used with delicate fabrics, such as silk. A nail head trim has a masculine quality and is used with heavier upholstery materials, such as leather. On most upholstered items the choice between gimp and nail heads will be a matter of preference. Gimp is easily applied and is good for sprucing up projects at home. It can be used to trim the top and bottom of lampshades or can be glued along the edge of shelves to add a decorative touch.

A **LINE OF COLOR** is a quarter-inch to half-inch of fabric in a contrasting color that is sewn into the edge of a primary fabric as a trimming. The fabric used for a line of color is typically thin cotton or silk. A solid chintz fabric is very suitable. A line of color is a subtle trimming that is simpler than cord or fringe. The edges of a tablecloth, the bottom edge of a bedskirt, the front and bottom edges of curtains, and the bottom edge of a valance are suitable places for a line of color. Lampshades often have a line of color.

NAIL HEAD TRIM is a decorative finish used to conceal upholstery tacks at the line where the fabric meets the wood frame on a piece of furniture. Nails can be used instead of gimp and they come in a few finishes: shiny, antique, or spotted. An antique finish is muted and usually better suited to older pieces of furniture. A typical place to see nails is on a leather chair in a study, but they can also be used on dining room chairs with tapestry, or on a bergère with a toile, for example. It is possible to use nails to create a decorative pattern along the side rails of a tight seat. This can be a great detail. Generally, it is not a problem to use nails on an antique piece; the wood will already have been nailed into for upholstery at some point so won't be damaged by doing it again. Occasionally, however, a frame is too delicate to use nails again.

ROSETTES are a silk trim resembling a round flower with loops of thread coming from the center. They are sewn into a buttoned seat cushion or into tufts.

TAPE is a flat, woven trim. It is applied to the front and bottom edge of curtains and also used as a trimming for valances. Tape is well used around the bottom of a bedskirt, a tablecloth, a sofa or chair skirt, or as a decorative detail on a throw pillow. It comes in varying widths and should be sewn, not glued, on.

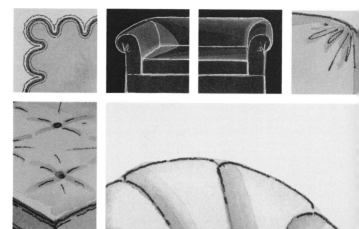

upholstery

9

In the mid- to late 1800s the coiled metal spring
was invented, making possible the all-upholstered
furniture that has become standard today. Before
then, furniture generally had an exposed wooden
frame with just the seat and back upholstered. ■
Upholstered furniture can be either custom-made
or ready-made, which is anything mass-produced.
While custom-made furniture is usually more expensive, it is also typically of higher quality and will last
longer than most ready-made furniture. There are
many manufacturers, though, who make top-quality
upholstery. ■ As long as you're dealing with rep-
utable sources, upholstery is an area where you get
what you pay for. When shopping for upholstery—
whether custom-made or ready-made—take into
consideration how it has been constructed.

Upholstery Construction

An all-upholstered custom-made piece of furniture starts with the frame. Upholsterers use a wood such as maple for frames, which is a good choice as it's hard enough to be strong and durable but also soft enough to nail into repeatedly. Webbing, typically made of jute, is stretched across the frame. Springs are attached to the webbing and are also tied with twine to each other. How tightly the springs are tied down will determine the height and the firmness of the seat. The springs in the seat are a heavier gauge than those in the back. The springs are covered with a layer of canvas or burlap and then a layer of thick filling material, which is often cotton. Historically horsehair and sometimes straw (in poorer construction) were also used for the filling. (Today horse or animal hair is used mostly in restoring antiques that were originally filled with it.) The filling layer is covered with muslin, which is a thin cotton fabric. The primary upholstery fabric is then applied over the muslin. Sometimes there is an added layer of padding between the muslin and the primary fabric.

A good frame can be nailed into and redone many times, but a weaker frame will fall apart when overworked. Instead of springs, a zigzag wire is sometimes used, which is a cheaper construction. The filling in some upholstery might be cardboard or cheap foam, both of which will not last many years. There is an argument that if you find a relatively inexpensive all-upholstered sofa or chair that you like and find comfortable, you buy it with the understanding that it won't last as long as a better constructed piece would. However, if you have the resources, a well-constructed all-upholstered sofa or chair is well worth the investment.

At flea markets and auctions it is possible to find old wooden upholstery frames. This can be a great way to have a piece of furniture made up. A piece of upholstered furniture in terrible condition that has a great frame—with an interesting shape and high-quality wood—is well worth stripping and re-upholstering.

Slipcovers

Slipcovers are so practical. They can be removed for cleaning and they can cover a less-than-desirable upholstery fabric. Slipcovers can be made to fit perfectly or they can be a little baggy on purpose to conceal the shape of the chair or sofa underneath. Baggy slipcovers have a slightly shabby chic flair to them and snug fitting slipcovers have a neater, cleaner look. Slipcovers can be made for sofas, chairs, or even headboards. If you have kids or pets, slipcovers are great.

If you have slipcovers custom-made, the furniture should be measured precisely. It is best if the person making the slipcovers measures the piece of furniture for him- or herself.

A light- to medium-weight fabric is best for slipcovers. It makes sense to use a fabric that can easily be washed or dry-cleaned. The classic slipcover that comes to mind is a solid colored cotton duck with a self-welt. A narrow welt should be used in making slipcovers. Other trimmings might not withstand washing or cleaning. To prevent slipcovers from shrinking, a good trick is to put them back on the chair or sofa while they are still a little damp. It's a good idea to wash or dry-clean all slipcovers in a room at the same time so they wear evenly.

Throw Pillows

Throw pillows present a great opportunity to add color and texture to a room. They are best used on a sofa or chair with a tight back, but can also be used on a sofa or chair with loose back cushions. A banquette can have a row of throw pillows instead of—or in addition to—an upholstered back. Throw pillows can make the deep seat of a sofa or chair more comfortable for a shorter person.

The top of the line—Rolls-Royce of throw pillows—is filled with 100 percent down. This is the softest, most luxurious, and also the most expensive filling. A mixture of down and feathers is also good but not quite as soft. Another option is a Dacron filling.

Throw pillows trimmed with fringe, cord, or tape jazz up a room and add decorative detail. Since throw pillows are relatively small, they offer a great chance to add a splash of beautiful material without spending a huge amount of money. The size and shape of throw pillows vary but should be proportional to the piece they are going on—a small pillow on a small piece, for example. There are a few different styles of throw pillows. An all-time favorite is an 18-inch square throw pillow with a knife edge, gathered corners, and a short fringe sewn in the seams. This pillow will take you anywhere.

BOX-EDGE PILLOWS are shaped like a box. They have sides that are typically 2 to 3 inches deep that connect the front and back pieces. The sides can be the same fabric as the front and the back or a contrasting fabric. The depth of the sides should be proportional to the size of the pillow; for example, a larger pillow will have deeper sides. A great look is to sew a short and bushy fringe in the seams. This requires twice as much fringe as trimming a knife-edge pillow. A box-edge pillow does not have gathered corners. A rectangular box-edge pillow in the center of a sofa looks great. Typically, loose sofa and chair cushions have a box edge.

GATHERED CORNERS are when the corners on the pillow are drawn into the pillow so that they are rounded and slightly pleated. This gives the pillow a softer, fuller look. Gathered corners are used with a knife-edge pillow.

KNIFE-EDGE PILLOWS have a single seam connecting the front and the back and do not have the sides that a box-edge pillow has. This pillow can either have plain or gathered corners. Plain corners have a more tailored look and gathered corners give the pillow a softer, fuller look. A fringe or a cord can be sewn into the seam, which is a good idea. It can be attractive to apply tape 2 to 3 inches from the edge on the front and the back.

Upholstered Furniture Details

ARM DETAILS will determine much about the style of an all-upholstered sofa or chair. If the arms extend the full depth of the seat, they are called full-depth arms. Other arms are not full depth; these are called setback arms and create a T-shaped seat cushion, which is illustrated with the setback arm on the following page. Arms can be the same height as the back; tuxedo sofas, Chesterfield sofas, knole settees, and many contemporary sofas and chairs have this design. Arms can also be lower than the back; Bridgewater and Lawson styles are examples of this. The arms can also have a variety of shapes. A scroll arm, illustrated below, is frequently seen. An alternative to a scroll arm is a square arm, which is often used in contemporary and modern design. A few more upholstery options for arms are detailed below.

Flat-Panel Arm is when the front vertical plane of the arm is upholstered with just one flat panel. Welting or cord can be sewn into the seam around the panel or the arm can be left untrimmed for a cleaner look. A flat panel arm can be on either a scroll arm or a square arm. It is versatile and used in many styles. Slipcovers have flat-paneled arms. It is the style with the least amount of detail.

Table Skirts

Making a table skirt for a simple unfinished round wooden table can be less expensive than buying a finished table. It is very suitable for a traditional setting. Such a table can

go anywhere, from a bedroom to a living room. It's best if the table skirt is lined with a fabric, such as cotton sateen; this makes it hang better and makes it look fuller. It's even better if the fabric is interlined with a layer of flannel between the primary fabric and the lining fabric. This will give it a softer, more luxurious look and will make it hang better. The skirt should be made to break one inch on the floor.

The unfinished tables are generally 27 to 30 inches high. The right diameter will depend on where the table is going. As a bedside table, the diameter might be 28 to 30 inches. In the corner of a living room, 34 to 36 inches, and as an end table next to a sofa, a good size is 30 to 32 inches in diameter.

There are a number of ways to jazz up a table skirt. Tape or fringe can be used around the bottom. Creating a shirred border along the bottom is an attractive detail. It's a good idea to get a piece of glass cut to fit the top of the table to prevent stains from plants or glasses.

Setback Arm does not extend the full depth of the seat. When a sofa or chair has a setback arm, the seat cushion has to have a T shape. Such a cushion is called a T-cushion. The alternative to a setback arm is a full-depth arm, where the arm extends the full depth of the seat.

Set-in Panel Arm has a flat panel set into the arm. The fabric is gathered around the panel, which is a nice detail that lends itself to trimming with cord, a welt, or nail heads. It has a rather traditional look.

Wrap-Around Arm has fabric that is pleated around the curve of the front vertical plane of a scroll arm. A wrap-around arm is best with a thin to medium-weight upholstery fabric such as chintz or linen. In this style, the arm does not call for trimming. It has a relatively simple look compared to a set-in panel arm.

BUTTONS can be sewn into a flat upholstered surface to help create a softer look. The buttons are covered in the upholstery fabric, a complimentary fabric, or can be a rosette. Typically you see buttoning on the loose seat cushion of a side chair, for example. Buttons can also be used on a tight seat. The look is similar to tufting, but the indentations or folds are not as deep.

CHANNELS create vertical sections in an upholstered back. This treatment lends itself in particular to the curved back of chairs. Channeling has an Art Deco flair. It has a more modern or contemporary look than tufting and creates a soft dimensional effect on a flat surface. Like tufting, channeling affects the pattern on a fabric. Small prints, weaves, or solid fabrics are generally better to use on a piece that will be channeled.

ENGLISH EDGE is when the tight seat of a sofa or chair projects a couple of inches over the platform of the seat. An English edge is typical of a Chesterfield sofa. An English edge can also be found on banquettes. It adds detail to a piece of furniture.

LOOSE BACK and **LOOSE SEAT CUSHIONS** are separate pillows set on an all-upholstered frame. It can be a more casual look than tight back upholstery as it is generally more comfortable, though the formality is really determined by the style of the piece of furniture and the fabric that it is covered in. The alternative to a loose back and seat cushions is a tight seat and

back, where there are no separate cushions (see page 175). Loose cushions with removable covers are most practical, as they are easily cleaned. Loose cushions make a sofa or chair squishier and easier to sink into than a tight seat and back. The downside is that cushions should be regularly fluffed after they have been sat on to look tidy. Cushions can be filled with a blend of feathers and down, which will be very soft but requires frequent fluffing up. It is common these days to fill cushions with poly-foam wrapped in feathers and down or Dacron, which helps the cushion keep its shape. It is possible to have a tight back with a loose seat cushion, but you would not have a loose back cushion with a tight seat.

PIPING or **WELTING** is a cord covered in fabric and set into the seams around the edges of seat cushions and around the arms of upholstered sofas and chairs. Piping is also used along the top seam of a sofa or chair skirt or a bedskirt. The piping can be in a complementary fabric or it can be covered in the primary fabric used to upholster the whole piece. It is called a self-welt when it is covered in the primary fabric. Piping, or welting, is more standard and universally used than a special cord trimming.

PLEATS add a nice detail to chair and sofa skirts, valances, lampshades, and bedskirts. Shirring, also called gathering, creates a ruffled effect that adds detail similar to a pleat. Something to keep in mind is that pleats and shirring both require more fabric than a flat or straight treatment. They also add dimension and detail. A few frequently used pleats are:

Box Pleats are flat, symmetrical, and used on the skirt of a sofa or chair, a bedskirt, a valance, or on a lampshade. These pleats are evenly spaced. The spacing of the pleats is optional but should be proportional to the size of the piece. On a sofa the pleats might be a little farther apart than on a smaller chair skirt. On a lampshade the pleats might just be an inch or so apart.

Inverted Single Pleats are also called Kick Pleats. They are typically used on a bed-skirt, a valance, or a chair or sofa skirt. Usually they are used at the corners of a piece, but also sometimes in the center of a skirt of a long sofa to conceal a seam.

Inverted Double Pleats, like inverted single pleats, are typically used on the corners of a bedskirt, a valance, or a chair or sofa skirt. They have two folds, as opposed to an inverted single pleat, which has just one fold. Unlike the invert-ed single pleat you are not likely to use it at the center of a skirt on a long sofa. Inverted double pleats are a bit more detailed than an inverted single pleat. They are best made with thinner fabrics. An all-upholstered sofa or chair that is covered in chintz, for example, would be well suited to a straight skirt with inverted double pleats at the corners.

Knife Pleats are flat, narrow, and closely spaced pleats that are folded in the same direction. These pleats are typically seen on lampshades although it's possible to use them with a light-weight fabric on a skirt.

SCALLOPED EDGE adds a bit of decorative detail that can be great on curtains, valances, throw pillows, and any soft goods including tablecloths and bedspreads. The size of the scal-lop should be proportional to the piece it is on. Scallops are a particularly pretty detail for the edge of a bedspread.

SCROLLBACK creates a curve at the top of the back of a sofa or chair that projects beyond the line of the back. A scrollback, which is a traditional detail, might be seen on a slipper chair, for example. It's a detail that adds shape and dimension to a piece of furniture and is used with a tight back, not a loose back cushion. Practically speaking, if you plan to put a sofa or chair up against a wall, there is no point to having a scrollback. This detail is best used when a chair or sofa will be placed away from a wall so the scroll can be seen.

SHIRRING is when fabric is gathered tightly on a rod, a thread, or a cord. It is sometimes referred to as "gathered" fabric and creates a ruffled effect. Shirred fabric is used for chair and sofa skirts, bedskirts, lampshades, curtains, valances, or even as a wall treatment. Shirring is also very attractive as a border around a headboard or a loose seat cushion with a box edge. This is a traditional detail with a very pretty look. Shirring adds texture and dimension. Do note, though, that it requires twice as much yardage to shirr medium- to heavyweight fabric and up to three times as much yardage for a sheer fabric.

SKIRTS are seen frequently on all-upholstered sofas and chairs as well as on bedskirts. The design details for skirts can also be applied to the design of a valance.

Choosing a skirt is really a matter of preference. The fabric will contribute to the look of a room more than the style of the skirt will. Typically a chair or sofa skirt starts 7 to 9 inches off the floor. A waterfall, or dressmaker, skirt is the exception: it starts at the top of the platform of the seat. (If you are using bullion fringe as a trimming, it takes the place of the skirt.) Piping, also called welting, or cord is generally sewn into the seams at the top of the skirt, and tape can be used along the bottom.

Skirts can be shirred, or gathered, all around, which creates a soft effect. They can be straight with no pleats, which is a very clean look. They can have more traditional box pleats, or they can be straight with inverted pleats at the corners, which is also a relatively clean look. Two additional styles are:

Straight Skirt with **Gathered** or **Shirred Corners** has a classic look that is a little less tailored than a straight skirt with inverted corner pleats and a little more tailored than a skirt that is shirred all around. It is best made with a light- to medium-weight fabric.

A **Waterfall Skirt,** also called a **Dressmaker Skirt**, is where the fabric falls from the top of the outside of the back and from the platform of a chair or sofa seat. This is a clean and classic look with no interruptions. A waterfall skirt will show more of the full pattern of the fabric.

SWIVEL BASES permit an all-upholstered chair to turn 360 degrees. This is very useful for pivoting to watch television in a living room or a library. When you have a chair or two on a swivel, the television does not have to be the focal point of a conversation grouping. It can be off to the side, and the chairs can be swiveled around as needed. The swivel mechanism is inserted into the base of the chair so the chair legs will be raised slightly off the ground. It is possible to put a swivel into a ready-made chair, which will increase your options with the furniture layout in a room.

TIGHT BACK and **TIGHT SEAT** on a sofa or chair means there are no loose cushions. This style of upholstery tends to be more tailored and cleaner looking than upholstery with loose cushions (see page 171). It can also be less comfortable, as there aren't thick, squishy pillows to sink into. It is generally a neater look than loose seat cushions as there are no cushions that need puffing. The look of the piece will also in great part be determined by its style and its fabric.

Tight backs on sofas and chairs lend themselves to throw pillows, which is great for added color in a room. If a tight back and seat are tufted, it adds dimension and detail. It is more difficult to clean spills on a tight back or seat than on a loose cushion, which can be sent out for cleaning or just flipped over. A sofa bed with a tight back means fewer cushions to remove and store when the bed is pulled out, and the back is more comfortable as a headboard.

TUFTING creates a series of evenly spaced diamond- or triangular-shaped sections in upholstered furniture such as sofas, chairs, ottomans, banquettes, and headboards. Each tuft is held with a button that is covered with the upholstery fabric, a complementary fabric, or a rosette. Tufting creates pattern and dimension on a piece of furniture. Certain styles of upholstery always use tufting: a Marshall Field chair or a Chesterfield sofa, for example. Keep in mind that tufting will distort the pattern of the fabric, so it's best to use a small print or a solid color. Like buttoning and channeling, tufting adds an interesting, soft detail.

Upholstered Furniture Styles

Upholstered furniture styles are somewhat standard, though the names will vary. With custom-made upholstery almost anything is possible. Below are some standard upholstery styles.

BRIDGEWATER UPHOLSTERED ARM-CHAIR or **SOFA** has medium to large proportions with curved arms. It is elegant and well suited to a living room, a library, or a bedroom. It can be upholstered with a tight seat and back, with loose seat and back cushions, or with loose seat cushions and a tight back.

CAMELBACK SOFAS have a serpentine profile along the top of the back. The eighteenth-century English cabinetmaker Thomas Chippendale designed sofas with this curve, and they are still sometimes called Chippendale camelback sofas. This design is better suited to a traditional or eclectic look than to a strictly modern or contemporary look.

CHESTERFIELD SOFA has a tufted seat, back, and arms and is often seen covered in leather. The Chesterfield sofa is a classic English design with a clubby look. A Chesterfield sofa is perfect in a library with wood-paneled walls, a fireplace, and lots of books.

LAWSON UPHOLSTERED ARMCHAIR or **SOFA** is a classic, popular style and can be finished in myriad ways. The arms are squarer than in the Bridgewater style. Lawsons can have a tight seat and back, loose seat and back cushions, or a loose seat cushion with a tight back. They can go in any room, from a formal living room to the corner of a bedroom.

MARSHALL FIELD ARMCHAIR has a curved, tufted back and a seat that is either tight and tufted or a loose cushion. It is an elegant chair because of the curves and looks beautiful covered in a silk damask trimmed with silk cord. This is a style that can go in the most formal of settings but also, in a less dressy fabric such as a cotton or linen weave, in a more casual setting.

ODOM UPHOLSTERED ARMCHAIRS have delicate proportions, a rounded front, and a relatively smaller scale than other styles. An odom armchair is great in the corner of a bedroom—it lends itself to a cozy look, especially if covered in a fabric with a small-scale print. It can also look very elegant, especially when covered in a fine fabric.

TUXEDO SOFAS have a back and arms of continuous height. The clean lines of the back and arms mean that a tuxedo sofa suits a contemporary look. The degree of formality depends on the fabric the sofa is covered in.

Creating an Asian Look

The Asian look is spare and uncluttered but radiates a rich simplicity. You can create the look in either a traditional or contemporary style. The living room might have a simple rectangular wooden coffee table with one beautiful object on it. Sofas and chairs with clean lines are well suited.

Elements that lend themselves to this look are silk fabrics, lacquered (or high-gloss) walls in beautiful rich colors, and natural materials such as wood, bamboo, and rattan. Grass cloth and tea paper are excellent wall coverings for this look. In a more formal setting, there are some beautiful Chinese hand-painted wallpapers. Floor covering can be wall-to-wall sisal or a wood floor covered with Tibetan or Oriental area rugs. Japanese paper lanterns can add a wonderful sculptural element.

In traditional Japanese design there is typically at least one natural element. A beam or a rafter may be left in the original form of the tree branch it is made from. In modern spaces this effect can be achieved by having tall branches such as cherry blossoms in a vase on a side table.

wall treatments

10

Choosing a wall treatment means thinking about color, texture, and pattern. Looking through a book of paint chips or a stack of wallpaper samples, the choices can seem endless. Start by thinking about the feeling you want in a room. White and pale colors create a light and airy atmosphere. Bright and bold colors create a surprise. Deep, rich colors are warm and cozy, especially in the evening. ■ If you have a lot of pictures to hang in a room, you'll want a background that won't compete with the pictures. If you don't have many pictures, you may want a patterned treatment to dress up the walls.

■ If you have walls covered in layers of old paint or wallpaper or even cracks, you may choose a wall treatment that will conceal the blemishes—such as upholstered walls. Start with spending the time and money to properly prepare your walls. And no matter which treatment you choose, consult an expert at a paint store on which products to use to work safely and achieve the best effect.

Ceramic Tiles

Ceramic tiles have been used throughout history on floors and walls. Different regions have developed their own traditional decorative tile designs. Delft tiles from the Netherlands, which have a white ground with a blue pattern, and pictorial tiles from the Mediterranean region are great in a country kitchen. There are also ceramic tiles from specific periods of design—Art Deco and Art Nouveau, for example. In traditional Spanish design ceramic tiles were widely used in the dado, or lower section of a wall. There are more utilitarian, machine-made, ceramic tiles frequently seen in bathrooms, kitchens, and laundry rooms. Tiles in general are extremely useful, especially in bathrooms and kitchens, as they are easy to maintain and are not damaged by water. Be aware, however, that wall tiles and floor tiles are different, and it's important to get the right one for your purpose. Wall tiles are generally thinner than floor tiles.

Mirror

Mirror can be successfully used as a wall finish. Panels, or sections, of mirror are affixed to the wall with an adhesive. The glass can have a clear, antiqued, or smoked finish. If you don't want a blast of glass, use an antiqued or smoked finish, which will have a softer, older look. In a utilitarian room, such as a closet or a bathroom, clear glass is better. The look of mirrored walls is modern and glamorous—like 1940s Hollywood. It goes well with martini glasses and stylish ashtrays. However, it can also be used to cover a wall in bad condition or old cracked tiles in a bathroom. Besides reflecting light, mirror also reflects whatever is across from it, so be sure it's worth looking at twice. You can hang pictures over mirror, which can be very chic and break up the surface. A mirrored wall can make a space seem bigger.

Paint

Paint is composed of pigment, which gives color; binder, which holds the pigment to the surface being painted; and solvent, also called the carrier, which allows the paint to be spread and then evaporates to let the paint dry. A paint type is named for its binder, so a latex paint has a latex binder.

It's easy to take for granted the enormous choice of paint colors we have today. The large selection is due to the development of man-made and synthetic pigments. Historically, natural pigments were the only option for color and the best, brightest, and most expensive colors were reserved for the best rooms in the house. In the early eighteenth century the first man-made color, Prussian blue, was invented. The palette of paint colors expanded over time. Certain stylistic periods, such as the Georgian or Victorian periods, are defined by the colors that were available and fashionable at the time. The color mauve is a synthetic pigment introduced in the 1850s that was all the rage during the Victorian period. In historic preservation or when trying to recreate a certain period look, it is important to consider the paint colors available at that time.

Paint comes in gloss levels that include, from shiniest to flattest, high gloss, semi-gloss, pearl or satin, eggshell, and flat or matte. Glossier paints are easier to wash but will highlight flaws in a surface. A high-gloss finish can have a great lacquered look, but if the walls aren't smooth then it's not worth it. In children's rooms, kitchens, or busy hallways prone to fingerprints, a semi-gloss or satin finish is preferable as it can be washed. The chalky texture of a flat finish is not easily washed, but it's a good choice if the walls have flaws. The trim and any woodwork is often painted with a slightly glossier finish than the walls and ceiling.

Paint can either be oil-based or water-based. Latex and acrylic paints are water-based, so they dry faster with fewer fumes. Alkyd paint is oil-based, which has a richer appearance and is longer lasting and more durable, but it takes longer to dry and creates more fumes as it does. Oil-based paint is generally used on areas that get a lot of wear and tear, such as doors and trim, and water-based paint for the walls and ceiling.

Picking Paint Colors

Be brave. If you want a bright green bedroom, then be bold and don't let anyone talk you out of it. Whether it's a bright and bold or a light and subtle color you're after, do give some careful consideration to the exact color that you choose.

Generally, a color will appear paler on a paint chip than when an entire room is covered in it. Light is always shifting and changing so that a paint color in one room will appear slightly different in another room. It's important to see the color dry on the wall in the room where you will use it. Paint a test area on a wall and observe it at different times of the day as the light changes. Paint colors can be custom-blended, so it's possible to bring a piece of fabric, for example, to be matched at the paint store.

DECORATIVE PAINT TREATMENTS add a unique detail to a room. There are many different techniques, and decorative painters tend to develop their own styles and methods of achieving certain results. You can also find many excellent how-to books and videos on decorative painting. The beauty of decorative painting is that if you want a textured finish for a wall, it allows much more control over the color than wallpaper does. Much decorative painting employs glaze, which is a translucent coating of color that can be either oil- or water-based. Glaze is applied over a base coat of paint to add depth to the color. Something to keep in mind is the final outcome of any painting project will depend heavily on the preparation of the surface. If you're taking the time and expense to create a beautiful surface, it is well worth the time and expense to thoroughly prepare it. Preparation generally includes scraping, sanding, and sometimes skim coating, which is adding a thin layer of plaster. Also, it's a good idea to talk to the experts at an art or paint supply store about specific products. Generally speaking, oil- and water-based products shouldn't be mixed.

Faux Stone and **Faux Wood Treatments**, which simulate the pattern of stone or the appearance of wood grain, can be very attractive. In the nineteenth century it was popular to paint the lower section of a wall in faux marble or faux stone blocks. Something to keep in mind with faux stone and wood is that they look best when you use them where real stone or wood might be. For example, you might really have a marble floor or door casing, but a marble door is unlikely. However, a faux wood door can be very attractive. Faux stone and wood are very successful on baseboards, door and window casings, mantels, and tabletops. Getting the technique down can take practice, so a decorative painter with experience should be hired if you want perfection.

A **Mural** is a decorative painting on a wall. There is a long tradition of mural painting—the earliest cave painting could be considered a mural, and the ancient Egyptians painted on the wall. In the twentieth century the Mexican painter Diego Rivera was known for his large-scale murals. An entire room, just one wall, or simply the wall above the dado can be painted with a mural. Murals are painted directly onto the wall or they are painted on canvas or paper then hung on the wall in sections. If a mural is painted on paper, it is not removable from the wall unless the wall is first covered in muslin, which becomes the backing for the mural and would be removed with the paper. If a mural is painted on canvas, then the canvas can be affixed directly to the wall and later removed. The subject matter can be anything—from historical scenes to rolling landscapes. The most brilliant thing about a mural is it will always be unique to the space it is in.

Stenciling creates a pattern with neat crisp edges that can be repeated over and over again. It can be done on the wall, the floor, or on furniture. Before wallpaper was readily available, stencils were used to create pattern on the walls. The stencil is a thin sheet of non-absorbent material, such as wax-coated cardboard, with a cut-out design. Paint, or stain, is brushed across the stencil using a brush with short, stiff bristles. Stenciling is a great do-it-yourself project and pre-made stencils (such as specific historic patterns that were used in early America, for example) are readily available. A stenciled wall or floor goes well with a Swedish or a country look. Stenciling can be done all over a wall or floor or just around the border. A painted wood floor with a stenciled design can be great in a country kitchen.

Stippling is a finish created with a special brush, called a stippling brush, which is used to lift up bits of glaze to create a pattern. The color of the basecoat shows through where the glaze has been removed. The colors of the basecoat and the glaze are often similar so the pattern is subtle. It is possible to use a rag or cheesecloth, which have a slightly coarser look, instead of a stippling brush. Stippling gives the wall an interesting texture and can be used anywhere. It's possible to do it yourself, but achieving an even pattern takes practice. There are wallpapers that mimic the stippled look, but they don't have the luster or depth that a real glaze has.

Strie is a glazed finish with a vertical textured, striped effect. In French *strie* means "streak." A coat of colored glaze is applied over a basecoat, then a dry brush, or steel wool, is dragged down the wall to create a pattern. Strie gives a room an elegant and formal look. It takes practice to make the lines straight and to make them appear continuous from ceiling to floor. Another technique is to do a layer of horizontal stripes over the vertical stripes to create a woven look. Many wallpapers mimic these looks, but a real glaze has more depth and luster than wallpaper.

Hanging Pictures

Pictures can be hung on their own, as a pair, or in a grouping. In a hallway, you might have a row of pictures. Hanging pictures in a grouping is a good alternative to just having them in a ring around the room at the same level. It's best if there is continuity within the grouping. To hang pictures this way, first lay the pictures down on the floor and work on the spacing and arrangement, then hang them accordingly.

To hang pictures on a wall you need a tape measure, a pencil, picture hooks, and a hammer. First, measure the distance between the floor and where you want the top of the picture frame. Mark the wall lightly with the pencil where the center of the top of the frame should be. Next, take the wire on the back of the picture frame and use the tape measure to pull on the wire, as if the picture were hanging. Measure the distance from the highest point of the wire to the top of the frame. If that measurement is, for example, 5 inches, then you will nail the picture hook into the wall 5 inches below the pencil mark you already made. If you are using a picture hook, note that it is the hook, rather than the nails you put in the wall, that the wire will hang from, so the distance will need to be adjusted accordingly.

Trompe l'Oeil, or "fool the eye" in French, is a technique that makes images appear to be real. It can create a false sense of space by tricking the eye into seeing depth that doesn't exist. The Romans used the trompe-l'oeil technique with mosaic tiles to create realistic images. Trompe-l'oeil paintings were popular in Italy during the Renaissance and Baroque periods in the sixteenth and seventeenth centuries. On a wall with no windows, a trompe-l'oeil window with a wonderful view of a Tuscan landscape can be painted. A trompe-l'oeil bookshelf with the spines of favorite books will make a room, or just an alcove, appear deeper. In a kitchen it could be amusing to paint trompe-l'oeil shelves holding baskets of fruit, a loaf of bread, and perhaps a housecat. A little imagination and creativity can have great results with this technique.

Shirred Fabric

Shirred fabric can be a great way to cover up walls in disrepair. This treatment adds texture, warmth, and soundproofing to a room. To shirr fabric on a wall, install metal rods along the top of the wall and above the baseboard. The fabric should be lightweight—a thin cotton fabric works well. A horizontal channel is sewn into the fabric at either end for the rods to go through. The fabric is then gathered along the rods. This wall treatment requires a lot of yardage to create a fully shirred effect but can be less expensive than repairing damaged walls. It has a cozy look.

Stone

Stone such as granite, travertine, marble, or limestone, in tiles or larger slabs, can be installed onto an entire wall or just the lower portion of the wall. This is a very clean look—an architectural favorite. From Classical architecture to the

Modern movement of the twentieth century, stone has been very successfully used on walls. Stone slabs on the walls are seen in some of the finest architecture. Marble has a formal look, while granite with a flamed, or rough, finish has a more rustic look. Travertine has a wonderful texture and neutral color that varies from a pinkish to yellowish tone. Limestone also has a great texture that sometimes includes plant and animal fossils. If there is a stone countertop in a kitchen, the stone can be continued onto the wall to create a backsplash, which is the surface above a countertop that protects the wall. Travertine on the walls is well suited to a pared-down setting. From a bathroom to an entry hall to a living room, stone on walls is a classic and timeless look.

Upholstered Walls

Upholstered walls are padded and make a room very cozy. They are also great for keeping sound levels down. To upholster walls, you staple fabric over batting that is covered with a thin layer of cotton, felt, or Dacron. A trim of gimp should be used to conceal the line where fabric is stapled to the wall. This is a great way to cover up a wall in bad condition. The fabric can be anything that is sturdy enough for upholstery. Since it will be more difficult to wash than a painted wall, it's a good idea to choose a fabric that will conceal fingerprints near wall switches and such. Upholstering a wall is labor intensive but could be a do-it-yourself project. It's something a little different that can be a great addition.

Wainscoting

Wainscoting is woodwork applied to walls. It can be used on just the lower section of the wall, creating a dado, or on the entire wall. It is a classic wall treatment.

BEADBOARD has narrow wooden slats with grooves and beading between them. It was often used in the American Shingle style in the early 1900s and has a look that can be both informal and elegant. It can be used on just the lower third of the wall to create a dado or it can cover the entire wall. Beadboard adds texture to a surface and suits a country house or a cottage perfectly. It helps to protect walls in places like hallways and mudrooms where there's a lot of traffic.

WOOD BOARDS have a less formal look than traditional wood paneling and are well suited to a country or rustic setting. Wood boards, like wood paneling, provide some insulation and give texture to a wall. Generally, pine planks about 6 to 10 inches wide are used. The boards can be painted, stained, or left natural and just sealed. The plank can cover the entire wall or just the dado. This treatment is more expensive than just painting the walls, but if budget allows, it can look great and cover up walls that are in disrepair. It adds character and warmth. There are salvage shops where you can find old boards suitable for this wall treatment or new boards can be used.

WOOD PANELING historically provided insulation and the opportunity for carved, often elaborate, decorative detail. Many older rooms, especially in Europe, had painted paneling in pale colors, such as gray, blue, and green. Woods such as cherry, mahogany, oak, and pine are used for paneled rooms. The wood is either stained, oiled, and waxed or else it is painted. Either an entire wall can be paneled or just the lower section of a wall.

Boiserie is the name of a particular style of carved wood paneling seen in seventeenth- and eighteenth-century France that was often painted and gilded. It is quite ornate. When budget permits, wood paneling is one of the best traditional wall treatments and, depending on the style of the paneling, can also be great in a contemporary setting. The style of the paneling is ideally compatible with the architectural style of the house, and historically the styles of wood paneling changed with the architectural styles. Wood paneling is often available now in specific styles such as Colonial or Georgian, for example.

A less expensive method of creating a paneled look is to use applied molding, where moldings such as an astragal—a thin molding used in Classical architecture—are affixed to the wall in squares and rectangles to create the appearance of panels. This will help define space and add detail to the walls in a larger room.

Wallpaper

Wallpaper became popular in mid-eighteenth-century Europe. This was due in part to the availability of affordable wallpaper. Jean Baptiste Reveillon opened a wallpaper factory in Paris at that time. His designs were made using woodblocks that are still used and copied today. Until the late nineteenth century, wallpaper came in small panels, not rolls.

Wallpaper adds pattern, texture, and detail to a wall, but to buy and hang it is more expensive than painting. Wallpaper will give a room a snappier look than a plain painted wall. Keep scale in mind when choosing a wallpaper pattern. You don't want a huge print in a tiny room, or vice versa. An alternative to wallpaper is to hang fabric on the walls like wallpaper. The fabric has to be paper- or acrylic-backed, depending on the type of fabric; there are companies that do this. As with wallpaper, flaws in the wall will show, so the wall must have a smooth finish.

BORDERS are bands of wallpaper hung at the top of a wall just under the crown molding or instead of crown molding. They are often used with wallpaper but can also go on a plain painted wall to add interest. The effect of a wallpaper border is much like molding. It defines a space and adds detail. It has a traditional look and could be used in any room. Borders range from a few inches in width to over a foot wide. Many wallpapers have complementary borders. There are some great borders designed for children's rooms that are a fun addition. A stenciled design can be used as an alternative to a wallpaper border. A border can also be hung about one third of the way up a wall instead of a chair rail.

GRASS CLOTH is paper-backed woven raffia or straw that is hung like wallpaper. Originally found in China, grass cloth was manufactured in Japan for years. It was first imported to the United States in the 1930s. Typically it is a natural color but can be dyed a variety of hues. Either way, it gives a wonderful natural-looking texture to a wall. Grass cloth has a Japanese look — rich in its simplicity. It goes well with a wide variety of styles and gives warmth and texture to a room.

SCENIC WALLPAPER depicts historic or pastoral scenes and traditionally is used to cover the wall above the dado, which is the lower section of the wall. The scale of scenic wallpaper is bold and most are hand-printed and therefore quite expensive. They became fashionable in France in the early nineteenth century. In the early to mid-nineteenth century, scenic wallpaper was often used in Europe and America. It has a stately and historic look that is perfect for dining rooms. It's possible to get just one panel of scenic wallpaper and hang it framed like a painting. Panels of scenic wallpaper can also be put onto folding screens. Zuber Inc., which was founded in 1797 in Rixheim, France, still makes panoramic scenic wallpaper by hand using the original woodblocks. In 1961 Jacqueline Kennedy put Zuber scenic wallpaper up in the White House, and it can also be seen in Gracie Mansion in New York City.

Wallpapering Details

Wallpaper rolls come in European and American sizes. A European roll is approximately 20 inches wide by 11 yards long, which is a total of 55 square feet. An American roll is typically about 27 inches wide by 5 yards long, which is a total of 33 square feet. The widths are generally standard, but the lengths can vary, so it's always important to double-check how many square feet are on each roll. Also, there are "single rolls" and "double rolls." A double roll is twice as long as a single roll.

The person who is hanging the wallpaper should measure the walls and calculate how many square feet are needed to determine how many rolls he or she needs for the job. This is done by multiplying the length by the height, in feet, and subtracting for areas that will not be covered, such as windows. If there is a repeat in the design, you may need some additional wallpaper. From there you determine how many rolls to order. Since the color can vary from dye lot to dye lot, you want all the rolls of wallpaper to come from the same dye lot. It's even a good idea to order an extra roll or two from the same dye lot in case a wall or ceiling is damaged and needs to be patched.

TEA PAPER is a silvery color and was originally used to line Chinese tea canisters. The use of tea paper for decorative purposes most likely originated when tea canisters were exported to Europe and the lining papers were admired. Today there is silvered wallpaper that comes in rolls, which is much like original tea paper. The metallic look is very elegant and dressy in a front hall or a dining room. Additional detail can be created using a glaze to stencil a design over tea paper. Tea paper can also be put on folding screens, which adds a metallic dash to a corner.

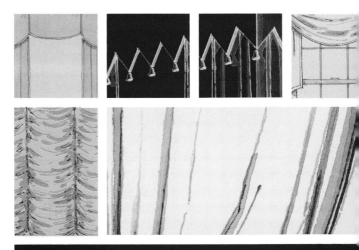

window
treatments

11

There are many options for window treatments from curtains to window shades to blinds to shutters to nothing at all. One thing to consider is that if you have an unappealing view or nearby neighbors, then blinds or shutters with louvers will allow in air and light while also providing privacy and partially concealing the outlook. If you like what you see out the window, then the window treatment should open to reveal the entire view. ▓ Aside from the practical purposes of privacy, insulation, and light control, window treatments also help to establish the style of a room. Curtains and window shades can range from elaborate and formal to simple and informal. The fabric they are made from will have much to do with their look. Shutters and window blinds have a streamlined design and are highly versatile. ▓ Some windows open inward, which will affect your choice of window treatment.

Blinds

Blinds are horizontal slats of wood or metal held together by plastic or cotton tape and controlled by a cord. They are sometimes called Venetian blinds. The slats can be tilted to control light and air flow, making them versatile and practical. If you don't like the view out your window, blinds can partially conceal it while also letting in air and some light.

Blinds with wooden slats are called wood blinds. Typically wood blinds are stained, but they can also be painted to match the wall color in a room. Wood blinds lend themselves to a variety of looks—Asian, country, or urban sophisticated. Their clean natural look suits both traditional and contemporary design very well.

Curtains

Curtains were historically used for insulation, for privacy, to regulate light, and to make a window look finished. The emphasis today, with the advent of central heating, is less on insulation and more on decorative value. Deciding on the right design for curtains starts with taking the architecture, style, and formality of the room into consideration. In a room with substantial architectural detail, curtains are more likely to be elaborate. Simpler architectural detail dictates a simpler curtain treatment.

When buying or designing curtains, it's a good idea to allow a half inch or so of extra length, measuring from where the top of the curtain will go to the bottom of the hem. If the floor is not perfectly even, the extra length will ensure that there is no gap between the curtains and the floor. Historically, for purposes of insulation, curtains broke 6 to 8 inches on the floor, meaning the curtains had extra fabric that puddled there. Today, a 1- to 4-inch break is used in formal treatments.

Trimming — whether it is cord, fringe, tape, or a line of contrasting color — adds interest and detail to curtains. Store-bought curtains can be spiced up with trimmings to make them look custom-made. Curtains either hang on a pole with rings or draw on a traverse rod, also called a track. It's possible to have stationary curtains that don't draw. This requires less fabric, but means the curtains will just be decorative.

In tight quarters, it can be a good idea to use curtains instead of a closet door. The curtains, especially if they are in a lightweight fabric, will not take up as much space as a door.

INTERLINED CURTAINS have a layer of flannel between the primary fabric and the lining fabric, which is often a cotton sateen. Flannel helps the curtains to hang more luxuriously and provides additional insulation. When budget allows and you want substantial curtains, consider interlining. Curtains can also be interlined with blackout lining, to create a completely dark room. When using a blackout lining, it's important to make the valance the same way so the look is consistent.

LINED CURTAINS have a layer of fabric, which is often white or beige cotton sateen, sewn behind the primary fabric. The lining gives the curtains body and helps protect the primary fabric from sun bleaching. It is possible to use a contrasting lining fabric such as a small muted pattern. One thing to consider is that the curtain linings will be visible from the exterior of the house. Also, when light shines through the curtains, the color of a lining fabric can affect the primary fabric. With a colored lining fabric, it is best if the curtains are interlined (see above).

SHEERS are curtains that permit natural light to come through. Before central heating, one purpose of curtains was to help maintain a room's temperature. Since insulation is no longer a primary purpose for curtains, sheers have become more widely used. Historically, sheer curtains, called casement curtains or inside curtains, were hung behind full length "over draperies." Today sheers are mostly used on their own.

Sheers hang on a pole with rings or with ties, or else they draw on a traverse rod, which is also called a track. Sheers can be floor length or stop at the windowsill. They are great in bedrooms as they allow for privacy but also let in some morning light. Nothing is fresher and prettier in a country house than dotted Swiss sheers to the windowsill. Sheers have a soft and filmy effect, and full-length sheers are best when they are very full so they blow in the breeze. Sheers have become an integral part of a contemporary look—from bedrooms to living rooms. You could put a roller shade under sheer curtains to keep the light out when necessary.

UNLINED CURTAINS have no lining but are not necessarily sheer. They billow in the breeze and have a wonderful soft look. They should be very full using a lightweight fabric such as silk or thin cotton. Heavier fabrics require lining and interlining to hang well, but thin unlined fabrics have a light and airy look. Unlined silk curtains on a pole with rings are a particular favorite.

Curtain Details

CURTAIN POLES come in a variety of sizes and finishes, from polished wood to wrought iron to brass. They can vary from a thin metal pole to a heavier wood pole. They either have finials at the ends or else return to the wall, illustrated here. Curtain poles that return to the wall are a little cleaner looking, and those with finials are a little dressier. Wooden curtain poles can be painted, stained, or gilded to suit the look of the room.

The alternative to a curtain pole is a traverse rod, also called a track. On a curtain pole with rings, the curtains are opened and closed manually. On a traverse rod, they draw on a pulley mechanism operated by a cord.

A **PLEATED HEADING** is necessary to gather the fabric at the top of a curtain. It conceals the traverse rod when the curtains are closed. Curtains on a pole with rings will also sometimes have a pleated heading. There are quite a few types of headings, below are two favorites:

French Pleats, also called Pinch Pleats, have three pleats gathered and stitched together at the base. This method is especially good with lightweight fabrics.

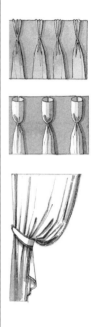

Goblet Heading, or Cartridge Heading, is a heavier single fold. This is a good option with a heavier fabric, as there is just one pleat rather than multiple pleats.

TIE-BACKS hold curtains open and can be made from the same fabric as the curtains, a complimentary fabric, or a cord and tassel. They are secured to a hook on the wall behind the curtains. Instead of fabric or cord, a tie-back can also be a decorative piece of metal hardware that is installed directly onto the wall. Before installing a tie-back, carefully consider at what height you want the curtains to be held back. There is no hard and fast rule. Generally speaking, tie-backs are often placed at approximately the top of the lower third of the curtain, but you will have to see what looks best in each situation.

The **TRAVERSE ROD**, also called the Track, is what curtains draw on. It has a cord that is pulled to open and close the curtains. The alternative to a traverse rod is a curtain pole with rings, along which the curtains are pulled manually. Curtains are affixed to the traverse rod with curtain hooks, which secure into the pleated heading of the curtains.

A traverse rod can be attached to the wall on brackets or installed directly onto the ceiling. The pleated fabric heading at the top of the curtains will conceal the traverse rod when the curtains are closed. When the curtains are open, the rod will be visible. A valance or pelmet is often used to conceal the traverse rod. For bow and bay windows, it can be curved to fit their curves.

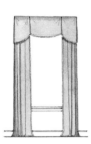

A **VALANCE** is a horizontal element that covers the top of curtains and conceals the traverse rod. Valances are shaped, lined, interlined, and trimmed to go with the curtains they cover. There are as many design options for valances as there are for curtains.

A window can be made to look taller or wider if a valance is placed high above the window or extends wider than the window. A valance is best used in rooms with a relatively high ceiling and should be made proportional to the height of a curtain. The trimmings should be carried to the front and bottom edges of the curtains below. A valance is installed onto a board which has been attached to the wall. It can be secured to the board using either tacks or Velcro. Velcro is preferable as the valance can be more easily removed for cleaning. If you have inward-opening windows, a valance will have to be carefully planned so the tops of the windows don't hit the bottom of the valance. A few variations of valance are:

A **Lambrequin** is a shaped board that covers the top and sides of a window frame. It can be finished wood or upholstered and simply used on its own without curtains underneath. There are many different shapes to choose from. It can replicate the shape of an onion dome for a Turkish or a Moorish look, or it can have a simple square shape. A lambrequin with a wood finish can be stenciled with a design. A tassel or two can be added for detail. A lambrequin is suitable on a window over a staircase, in a dining room, or in a hallway. Since it is stationary, you won't be able to control light and privacy unless you install a spring roller shade behind it.

Pelmet is a stiff shaped valance. It is made using wood or buckram, which is a stiff, coarse cloth. There are many design options with a pelmet. A favorite is a series of downward points trimmed with tassels. With pelmets, as with all valances including lambrequins, there should be an odd number of points, curves, or any design detail, so that one is centered in the middle of the window.

Swag and Jabot is a soft and elegant style of valance. Swags are horizontal drapes of fabric. Jabots, which means "ruffles" in French, are the vertical loose tails that hang over the curtains. There can be one or multiple swags, depending on the size of the window. The fabric of the swag and jabots can match or compliment the curtain fabric; alternatively the jabot can be lined in a contrasting fabric. Generally, swags and jabots are appropriate window treatments for formal rooms where the ceilings are high. In rooms with low ceilings, this treatment can look disproportional. Softer fabrics, such as silks or cottons, lend themselves to better draping than heavier fabrics. The curtains underneath should be floor length.

Shades

Window shades should ideally be installed into the reveal of the window so that the head rail is concealed. The head rail is the part of the shade that is affixed to the wall. If they must be installed on the window trim, you will want to conceal the head rail with a valance. Many shades come with their own simple valance.

AUSTRIAN SHADES are unlined fabric shades traditionally made with lightweight silk. They are swagged in sections and trimmed with a small ruffle or fringe. Traditionally, Austrian shades were used under curtains and a valance. They are dressy and seen in formal situations—an embassy, a restaurant, or a living room, for example. You are also apt to see Austrian shades in a period room done to a particular style. Take note that since the shades are so full, a sizable portion of the window will be covered. Also, they require many yards of fabric.

BALLOON SHADES are fabric shades, lined or unlined, that are somewhat less formal than Austrian shades. They have a soft balloon shape and can be made with a lightweight cotton or silk fabric. Silk balloon shades with fringe would be rather fancy, while printed cotton balloon shades with no trim or a simple tape would be less fancy and could go in basically any room. Lining will protect the shade from sun damage.

BAMBOO SHADES have a wonderful warm color. They have a natural look and are versatile— suiting everything from an Asian look to a country look. Bamboo has been used for thousands of years. It is a type of grass with a hollow stem. Besides being used for window shades, it is also used to make paper, furniture, and flooring; the shoots are even served in most Chinese restaurants. From a city apartment to a house in the country—and everywhere in between—bamboo shades are a great addition. The shades can either be Roman or roll-up.

PLEATED SHADES are a relatively recent design where a single piece of fabric is folded into approximately one-inch horizontal accordion pleats. The fabric is synthetic and can be opaque or translucent. An interesting feature is they pull up from the bottom or down from the top. A pleated shade can cover the lower section of a window and let light in from the top or conversely it can cover the top section of the window and let light in the bottom. Where privacy is an issue, such as on the ground floor, pleated shades are a great solution.

ROMAN SHADES stack into neat folds that are approximately 6 inches wide. It is a design that has been used for centuries and can be made with fabric, bamboo, or woven wood. This style of shade is suitable for a contemporary or a classic look. The neat folds and slim design are tailored, and, when they are pulled all the way up, create a valance effect. Woven wood or bamboo has a natural country look and a silk fabric has a more formal look. Any fabric that is suitably durable can be used, from a cotton print to a heavier

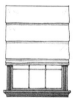

woven fabric. They are perfect in a bay window, or any tight space where a curtain rod is difficult to install. If Roman shades are made with fabric, they should be lined and can also be interlined. They hang best when they are interlined. Also they can be made to hang perfectly straight or to have a permanent pleat at the bottom. A cleaner look is to have the shade hang straight, but it's an added detail to see a pleat when the shade is down.

ROLL-UP is a style of shade frequently used with woven wood or bamboo or a substantial fabric such as canvas. An advantage is that roll-up shades don't take up much space at the top of the window as Roman shades do. This is something to consider if there is a beautiful view. In the Swedish style, you will see simple unlined cotton roll-up shades. These can be very pretty. When choosing between roll-up and Roman shades, the deciding factor is whether you want to see a roll or an accordion stack at the top of the window.

SPRING ROLLER SHADES have a mechanism that snaps the shade up into a roll at the top. The material can be anything from paper to vinyl to blackout material meant to block daylight. Paper and vinyl spring roller shades are one of the most economical window treatments. They are often installed under curtains, or other forms of window treatment, for light control.

SOFT ROMAN SHADES have a single swag at the bottom and hang flat when they are down. They are a simple and pretty shade that is seen often in contemporary design. They can be made with a sheer fabric to create a barely there window treatment, or they can be made with an opaque fabric and still have a pared-down feeling. This shade is suitable for traditional and contemporary styles. It is so straightforward that it can go basically anywhere.

WOVEN WOOD SHADES add color and texture and a natural element to a room. They suit many different styles—from city to country, Asian to contemporary. They also work in a variety of rooms, including a bedroom, a library, or a dining room. Woven wood shades can be made as Roman or roll-up shades.

Shutters

Shutters are hinged panels that cover a window. They can be louvered or solid, and they can be full length or double hung, meaning they break at the sash of the window. Before glass panes, shutters alone were used in windows for security and protection from the elements.

Movable louvers allow air to circulate while providing privacy and some measure of light control. The width of louvers will vary, and they should be proportional to the size of the window or door. Wide louvers should go on relatively large windows. Shutters with 3- to 4-inch-wide louvers are called plantation shutters. When open, wider louvers expose more of the view out the window than narrow louvers. Shutters are highly versatile and are suitable in any design style. They are simple and highly practical.

Some older houses were constructed with deep reveals at the windows that were fitted with built-in shutters. This is a very nice detail as the shutters fold back into recessed pockets. It is preferable to install shutters into the reveal of a window, but if this isn't possible they can be installed in a frame on the face of the window trim.

Measuring for Window Blinds and Shades

For shades and blinds to fit correctly, the window must be carefully measured. Some window treatment companies will send professionals over to measure for you—this is the safest bet. If you do it yourself, be sure to follow a few basic guidelines. It is recommended that you use a metal tape measure and be as accurate as possible. Also, check first with manufacturers on how to measure for specific products.

The first decision is whether the shades or blinds will be mounted on the inside or the outside of the window frame. Whenever possible try to mount window treatments on the inside. The depth of the reveal, which is the cross-section of the wall that is exposed, will determine whether or not you can do this. Different shades and blinds require different depths of the reveal, so you will have to check. The width of the window frame should be measured at the top, middle, and bottom in case there are inconsistencies. The length should be measured from the top of the window to the windowsill on both the left and right sides.

Window treatments mounted on the outside of the trim should take into consideration the architectural detail of the casing.

For roller shades, it is necessary for the shade to be longer than needed to cover the window so that some fabic remains on the roller.

Historical Style Index

AMERICAN COLONIAL PERIOD refers to the seventeenth and eighteenth centuries when America was still a colony of England. Architecture had a simple utilitarian design. Compared to Europe, early American style was based more on necessity, using local materials. The style integrates English and European influences and was concurrent with the Georgian period in England. Colonial Williamsburg in Virginia is an entire Colonial town.

ART DECO was seen in the 1920s and '30s, between World War I and II. The name comes from the Exposition Internationale des Arts Décoratifs et Industriels Modernes in Paris in 1925. Geometric designs and bright colors were typical. The Chrysler Building in New York City is a prime example, and in South Beach, Miami, the Art Deco style was widely used and has been restored in recent years.

In the **ARTS AND CRAFTS MOVEMENT**, during the late nineteenth and early twentieth centuries, the focus was on craftsmanship. Interiors were handmade using traditional methods where possible. English designer William Morris was its most famous practitioner.

ART NOUVEAU, or "new art" in French, was seen in the late nineteenth and early twentieth centuries in Europe and the U.S. Distinctive asymmetrical lines and organic forms are typical of this style. The Spanish architect Antoni Gaudi and early works by the Scottish architect Charles Rennie Mackintosh were influential in Art Nouveau.

BAROQUE STYLE was first seen in the late seventeenth century in Europe. It was characterized by elaborate ornament and opulence. St. Peter's Cathedral in Rome and Versailles in France are examples. St. Paul's Cathedral in London is also an example of Baroque architecture. In Quito, Ecuador, the city center is built in the Baroque School of Quito style and is a UNESCO World Heritage site.

The **EMPIRE PERIOD** was in the early 1800s during the reign of Napoleon in France, but it was also seen elsewhere. Egyptian motifs and Classical influences were common. The Empire style is quite grand.

FEDERAL PERIOD, an American style, came about shortly after the Declaration of Independence was signed. Neoclassical influences were seen. Duncan Phyfe, a Scottish-born American, was a particularly well-known cabinetmaker at this time.

The **GEORGIAN PERIOD** is divided into early Georgian and late Georgian. In England the reign of King George I began in the early eighteenth century, and the late Georgian period was late eighteenth and early nineteenth centuries, during the reign of King George III. The English cabinetmakers Thomas

Chippendale, George Hepplewhite, and Thomas Sheraton were designing furniture during this time. In early Georgian design cabriole legs and ball and claw feet were typical. Neoclassical elements define late Georgian style.

The **GOTHIC PERIOD** was approximately mid twelfth century to the beginning of the sixteenth century. Windows with pointed arches, flying buttresses, and elaborate tracery are typical. Chartres Cathedral and Notre Dame Cathedral in France and Westminster Abbey in England are examples of Gothic architecture. The Brooklyn Bridge in New York City has Gothic-style pointed arches.

The **MODERN MOVEMENT** in architecture developed in the twentieth century. There are a number of different styles and influences within the Modern movement, but an overall simplicity and scarcity of ornament or molding runs through all. The lines in the architecture and decoration are clean.

NEOCLASSICAL STYLE, in the mid-eighteenth and early nineteenth centuries, was inspired at least in part by the discovery of the ruins at Pompeii. Classical Greek motifs, rectilinear lines, and Classical forms were widely seen. The Scottish architect Robert Adam was particularly influential at this time. Neoclassical elements are seen during the late Georgian and Regency periods in England and during the Federal period in America.

REGENCY PERIOD, in early nineteenth-century England, refers to the period when George, Prince of Wales, was a regent before becoming King George IV. Classical design was often used and proportions were smaller than had previously been seen during the Georgian style. The English architect Sir John Soane's work is associated with the Regency style.

ROCOCO lasted for approximately 35 years in the early to mid-eighteenth century during the reign of Louis XV of France. The name Rococo is derived from the French words rocaille, meaning "rock," and coquille, meaning "shell." The shell motif was often seen as well as asymmetrical lines, curved shapes, and gilding.

TUDOR STYLE refers to the Tudor period of sixteenth-century England, during the reigns of Henry VII, Henry VIII, Edward VI, and Mary VI. These monarchs were all from the Tudor family. Characteristics of the style include whitewashed plaster between wooden supports on the exterior and oak paneling on the interior. Hampton Court Palace in England is a typical example of Tudor architecture on a grand scale.

The **VICTORIAN PERIOD**, during the reign of Queen Victoria of England, was in the mid- to late nineteenth century. There is a British Victorian and an American Victorian style. Both combined and revived historic styles such as the Gothic. American Victorian was influenced by England but also showed some European influences. Gingerbread architecture, mansard roofs, and dark wood and heavy trimmings on the interior were typical.

INDEX